Born in Melbourne and educated in Sydney and London, Peter Coleman was editor of the *Bulletin* in the 1960s and of *Quadrant* for twenty years. His books include a history of Australian censorship, *Obscenity Blasphemy Sedition*, the biographical studies, *The Heart of James McAuley* and *The Real Barry Humphries*, and an examination of the Cold War, *The Liberal Conspiracy: The Struggle for the Mind of Postwar Europe*. He has also edited several books, including *Australian Civilisation* and *Cartoons of Australian History* (with Les Tanner). He has served for some years in the Australian and New South Wales Parliaments, on the Board of the National Institute of Dramatic Art (NIDA) and as chairman of the council which established the Australian Film, Television and Radio Training School. His most recent book was *Bruce Beresford: Instincts of the Heart*.

MEMOIRS
OF A SLOW LEARNER

PETER COLEMAN

Angus&Robertson
An imprint of HarperCollins*Publishers*

An Angus & Robertson publication
Angus & Robertson, an imprint of
HarperCollins *Publishers*
25 Ryde Road, Pymble, Sydney NSW 2073, Australia
31 View Road, Glenfield, Auckland 10, New Zealand

First published in Australia in 1994.

Copyright © Peter Coleman 1994

This book is copyright.
Apart from any fair dealing for the purposes of private study, research,
criticism or review, as permitted under the Copyright Act,
no part may be reproduced by any process without written
permission. Inquiries should be addressed to the publishers.

National Library of Australia
Cataloguing-in-publication data:

Coleman, Peter, 1928-
Memoirs of a slow learner

ISBN 0 207 18248 5

1. Coleman, Peter, 1928- . 2. Legislators – Australia – Biography. 3.
Authors, Australian – 20th century – Biography. 4. Editors – Australia –
Biography. I. Title 328. 94092

Cover illustration by Robert Hughes
Printed by McPhersons Printing Group, Australia.

9 8 7 6 5 4 3 2 1
99 98 97 96 95 94

Contents

Foreword viii

PART ONE: **Growing Up Radical**
1. 'Divorce is an ugly word, Norman!' 3
2. Messages from the Underground 17
3. In the Re-education Centre 37

PART TWO: **Drifting**
4. London: 'Piccadilly Bushmen' 55
5. Khartoum: 'Only connect ...' 65
6. Canberra: Looking for a Life-belt 73

PART THREE: **A Fiddle for Eighteenpence**
7. Starting a New Magazine 89
8. New Critics 98
9. Cold War 118
10. Competitors and Allies 130
11. Last Days 141

PART FOUR: **Debacle**
12. God and Man in Sydney 155

For Tanya, William and Ursula

Some like me are slow to learn;
What's plain can be mysterious still,
Feelings alter, fade, return,
But love stands constant in the will.
                    James McAuley

Foreword

Scribblers, eggheads, blue stockings, chattering class—the intellectuals have always had a bad name wherever two or three people are gathered together who speak English, not least in Australia. They are self-indulgent windbags, opportunistic adventurers, unprincipled, faithless, godless.

Many who have passed their lives, openly or discreetly, in intellectual pursuits sometimes try to disguise their affliction under some other label—man of letters, philosopher, academic, humanist, freethinker, writer. None really fits the case, although *writer* being so vague comes close.

Yet there is more to it. The Athenian was surely right: the unexamined life is not worth living; and the Englishman was wrong: push-pin is not as good as poetry. Besides, once you have contracted the habit of looking behind the screen of life, once you are touched by the compulsion to examine conflicting values and ideas of the world, there is no turning back. As with painters or film directors, this unfortunate disposition usually emerges early in life and is impossible to cure.

It is often accompanied by what I once called Mill's Disease—the complaint described in the famous fifth chapter of John Stuart Mill's *Autobiography* when he recalls his mental crisis, what we would call breakdown, in the winter of 1826. He had for years found fulfilment in the mission of the freethinkers of his youth—the Philosophic Radicals—and their magazine, *Westminster Review*, but had now reached the belief that life was no longer worth living and that nothing could be done about it.

He knew his despair was not peculiar to him. Baudelaire later called it *spleen*. Heidegger called it *angst*. The modern poets write about very little else—and indeed it was Coleridge and the other

Romantics whose work helped Mill overcome his nausea. It is, I think, a common if not inescapable complaint of most secular intellectuals at some time or another.

Few knew this better than James McAuley, whose early Baudelairean cries of sterility are among his most moving work. But as he said much later in one of his autumnal poems, it is not true that we never learn: *Something is gathered in*—something worth preserving and passing on.

In these pages I try to shed some light not by formal argument but by taking these matters as they have affected me over the recent decades.

PART ONE

Growing Up Radical

For I dipt into the future, far as human eye could see,
Saw the Vision of the world, and all the wonder that would be;
Till the war drums throbbed no longer, and the battle flags were furled,
In the Parliament of man, the Federation of the world.

Tennyson

CHAPTER 1

'Divorce is an ugly word, Norman!'

It was not the weather you would pick for what amounted to an elopement. Melbourne was cold and wet on 8 January 1924 and there was snow on the highlands. But on the morning of that rainy Tuesday, as secretively planned for some weeks, Stanley Charles Coleman of East Malvern—24 years of age, born in Toowoomba, schooled in New Zealand, employed in the advertising department of the *Age*, short, dark, brown-eyed, in a grey two-piece suit and matching Akubra with turned-up brim and black band—stood, waiting outside 165 Collins Street.

His usually harassed features broke into a smile when at last his eye fixed on Norma Victoria Tiernan, also of East Malvern—20 years of age but purporting to be 21, born in Melbourne, schooled at the Presbyterian Ladies' College, employed as a book-keeper and wearing a frock of crêpe de Chine with contrasting colours on the bodice. Her blue eyes, so often distant and lost, returned his smile. Together they entered the Registrar-General's office where, having given due notice and duly made the required declaration, they were married.

In concluding the ceremony, the Registrar noted that the *Argus* itself had that very week described marriage as 'the greatest of life's contracts'. But nowadays, the *Argus* thought, too many young people entered on it 'thoughtlessly', unprepared to submit to its discipline. A little more 'solemnity' and a little less 'cynicism' were called for, the great newspaper declared, and the Registrar quietly but completely agreed.

My parents also agreed, in their way, with the *Argus*. My mother would have preferred to have entered matrimony according to Presbyterian or Church of England rites in East Malvern, where she had been born and raised. My father, an apostle of modernity as befitted his vocation of advertising, did not care one way or the other, since the Anglicanism of his fathers had become almost nominal. But he would have done anything to please my mother.

The problem was that a marriage in a church—in East Malvern or elsewhere—with all the ceremonial formalities would have involved the concurrence, if not cooperation, of my mother's parents. But my grandparents did not concur, and my grandmother in particular had made it clear beyond misunderstanding that she would never agree to her daughter marrying Stanley Charles Coleman, 'a blow-in from nowhere'.

After the contract in Collins Street, they took a train from Flinders Street to Stoney Creek and then the steamer to Cowes and 'the garden isle', which now boasted electric light and sewerage. For two weeks they forgot my grandparents and Melbourne.

Although little more than 80 years old, Melbourne in 1924 was a thrusting city of a million people. Suburbia was pushing south to the bay and east to the hills. New factories, protected by legislation, were opening almost daily. Traders were selling 1000 motor cars a month—Hupmobiles and Paige-Jewetts as well as Vauxhalls and Austins—and petrol pumps already outnumbered horse troughs in the city and suburbs. The new electric refrigerators in oaken cabinets were only five guineas. Radio receivers—with valves for best results: you could pick up Sydney's 2YG on New Year's Eve—were also selling briskly at £30. (Crystal sets with earphones were still only £2, but their range was weak.) A few things were free. If you presented the chemist with a newspaper coupon, he would present you with a tube of American toothpaste, which was useful in combating another American discovery called halitosis.

Melbourne was flocking in its hundreds of thousands to watch silent films in the new picture palaces. They could see Gloria Swanson as Swiftie in *Prodigal Daughters*, Pola Negri in *Forbidden Gardens*, Nazimova in *Salomé* and *Camille* (with Rudolph Valentino), Mary Pickford in *Tess of Storm County* or Florence Victor in Sinclair Lewis's *Main Street* proclaiming that she was sick of washing dishes: 'We're going to wash 'em by machines and come out to play with you men in the offices and clubs and politics!'

Why shouldn't they? Everything was changing. All around the world great emperors and sultans and kings had been toppled, terminated and tossed out. In Melbourne the Queen of Romania was a newspaper fashion consultant.

My grandmother's rage was unforgiving. When my parents finally returned to East Malvern to confront her—a short, thin, tight-lipped, iron-willed daughter of Tasmania—she spat at my mother: 'This will end in divorce!' Then turning to my grandfather, who took a less tragic view, she cried: 'Divorce is an ugly word, Norman!' She was already planning for one.

She had no words for my father. She had scorned his proposal and forbidden the marriage because Stanley Charles Coleman had neither money nor property nor family. 'Who is he? Where does he come from? Toowoomba! Nelson! Let him make his pile first!' Yet her daughter had ignored her advice, love and experience for the sake of a penniless nobody in advertising. They had even married in a registry office!

The young couple, happy despite my grandmother, moved into rooms in Elsternwick. My father got ahead at work. Some thought he drank too much, although that seemed to go with the job.

Gradually, day by day, week after week, my mother—supported by her father and her sisters—persuaded my grandmother to accept the calamity. They succeeded to the extent that, late in 1924 in time for Christmas, she reluctantly agreed to acknowledge that my father had become her son-in-law, provided the union were blessed by a Church of England minister.

A consenting clergyman was found and early in December, in the flower-decked drawing room of the family home, he conducted a short service of dedication to sanctify my parents' union. My grandmother called it a marriage ceremony.

My mother wore a bridal frock of brocade, with a pink-lined satin train and a veil of old Brussels lace secured, according to the Melbourne 'Chatter' column of the *Bulletin*, by a coronet of mixed pearls and orange blossoms. My grandmother stood throughout in a coal-black glitter of jet and sequins.

The guests were the Tiernan family, my mother's friends from PLC, grandfather's from business, and grandmother's from croquet and her women's groups. After the ceremony they moved on for a 'jollo' at the St Kilda Kiosk, a sort of Second Empire pavilion by the sea.

My father took along one or two colleagues from his office, including the editor of *The Leader*, a fellow Queenslander who served as 'best man'. Clutching around for a word to describe my father—on a page devoted to the activities of young men with grazing, stockbroking or vice-regal associations—the *Bulletin*'s columnist settled on 'young' Stanley Coleman.

My grandmother, appeased but not satisfied, confided to her other daughters: 'I hope there are no children.' But there were two. The first was called Norman after my grandfather.

By the time I was born in December 1928, the economic slump was turning towards the Great Depression. My father's bright future now suddenly became uncertain. Late in 1929, at the age of 30, he was sacked. Within weeks, as my grandmother predicted, his savings were gone . . . and with them, it seemed, his marriage.

His only offer of work was in New Zealand, where his brother had found him a job as a sporting journalist and general reporter on a Labour Party weekly newspaper. A desperate solution suggested itself. My humiliated father would join his brother in Wellington. My shattered mother would stay in Melbourne with her parents. To rescue something from the wreck of his youth, my father would take with him the apple of his eye, his first-born son. I, now two years old, would stay with my mother.

My parents put it about that, when everything was settled, we would all be reunited. No-one believed it. No-one went to see off the ship to New Zealand. The marriage had lasted a little over five years.

I grew up in Coppin Street, an oak-lined avenue in East Malvern that even now can still suggest something of the confident good times that Marvellous Melbourne recaptured in the years before the Great War. Our Queen Anne bungalow was then called 'Langi'—vaguely Scottish but chosen as an Aboriginal word meaning 'home of cicadas'. (The name and plaque were discarded by a later owner.)

The grounds (long since subdivided) boasted a summer house and a croquet lawn, and down the back black orpingtons strutted around a fowl run. (A slaughterman called every so often and we all laughed as headless chooks charged briefly around the yard or someone produced a warm egg from a dead bird and held it high like a magician.) There was also a horse and buggy, but the horse was stabled nearby.

Inside the house there were many rooms that a small boy dared not enter. There was a 'drawing room' with harps, cellos, a piano and a pianola. There was a stand-up, wind-up gramophone somewhere and a telephone on a wall. In a rare act of extravagance there were several wirelesses. There was only one book that I recall—a *Pears Cyclopaedia*.

In a huge kitchen adorned with a Philip's Commercial Map of the World, a 'live-in general' called Carrie helped my grandmother make vast supplies of jam and jelly from the plums and quinces of the garden. She could also be seen boiling clothes in a 'copper' with an attached wringer. There was a lattice and hessian fernery nearby which my grandmother kept watered as part of the gardening she loved. There was also a stream of delivery-men on horses-and-carts: a baker, an eggs-and-butter man, a fruit-and-vegetable man, an ice man who carried a block of ice in a sack on his shoulder, and a milkman who poured creamy milk into a billy.

The nominal head of this household was my grandfather, whose income was the rents of the various properties he had inherited and now managed. His grandparents—Thomas, a farmer from County Cork, and his wife Mary—were the 'original' Tiernans, arriving on the immigrant ship *Salsette* in Port Phillip on New Year's Day, 1841. Melbourne's population was about 5000 and the *Salsette* added another 188 souls. (Fourteen had died on the voyage—mainly infants, of 'inanition', or women, of various fevers including 'puerperal mania'. The Second Mate died of 'bilious fever' and a paying passenger of 'inflammatory fever'.)

The immigrants included blacksmiths, whitesmiths and gunsmiths; stonemasons, bricklayers and coopers; shoemakers, butchers and brewers; gardeners, millers, and printers; tailors, dressmakers and bonnet makers. There was even one lawyer. Most were married couples with children, but there were 17 single men and 28 single women. They were all bounty immigrants (costing £2703) and the English and Scots, unlike the Irish, were able to read and write. Thomas Tiernan was apparently a man of some spirit. In any case, the immigration agents advised His Honour Superintendant Latrobe of Port Phillip that Mr Tiernan had lodged a complaint on disembarking about the poor quality of the 'pease and ham' served on board.

He invested well if not shrewdly in property in the growing settlement and by the 1880s his eldest grandson—my grandfather—was attending the Jesuits' St Patrick's College, attached to the Catholic Cathedral, one of the few secondary schools in Victoria or indeed the Colonies.

At school my grandfather won a prize for Latin, which he kept out of sight in a cupboard of old papers and junk, but otherwise St Pat's did nothing to hold his loyalty or deepen his faith. He shunned its sodalities, attended none of its reunions and rarely attended church. When he married my grandmother, the service was Presbyterian and his three daughters were considered Presbyterians. When enrolling his oldest daughter in the Presbyterian Ladies' College he listed her as Methodist, perhaps because it was all the same to him.

He held to a lingering ethnic loyalty. During the Depression, men with names like Ryan or Bourke or Murphy would call at his back door looking for odd jobs on his properties. He always found them something, however footling.

He was not an active or enterprising man, not one to complain about 'the pease and ham'. He did not increase the family fortune (and he certainly did not volunteer for the Boer War). His characteristic position was in a rocking chair, pipe in mouth, spittoon nearby, one-and-nine penny spectacles on his nose, reading the *Argus*.

What else was there to read? He could never trust the *Age* with its wishy-washy softness on the high-tax Labor Party. The *Argus*'s reservations about the Irish (especially the immigrant Archbishop Mannix) occasionally irritated him, but otherwise it suited him: it opposed Mussolini as a man of violence, Franco as a rebel and Hitler as a threat to peace (although it despised pacifists and noted that a war might help our exports). It welcomed Neville Chamberlain's 'moral realism' at Munich. It deplored King Edward's infatuation with Mrs Simpson—how could a king possibly marry a woman with two divorced husbands?—and welcomed George VI and his heir apparent Elizabeth ('Lillibet'). It saw the British Empire as the one moral certainty in an unstable world.

My grandfather was a kindly, good-humoured man who, as far anyone in his 60s could, took over the task of fathering the small boy who had unexpectedly been presented to him. He took me to cricket matches and football practice, taught me how to sharpen a carving knife on a steel and sang me songs from his youth:

> 'Tis the last rose of summer left blooming alone;
> All her lovely companions are faded and gone.
> So soon may I follow when friendships decay,
> And from love's shining circle the gems drop away.

In his bowler hat, three-piece suit with a gold pocket watch, and black boots, he would stroll hand in hand with me through suburban streets as he checked his properties or did some shopping at the Chapel Street Chinese market—sometimes offering the child to the Chinamen for sixpence, to everybody's high amusement except mine. I have few warmer memories of these years.

But it was my grandmother who dominated 'Langi'—the 'head woman' as my grandfather called her. Born in Westbury, southwest of Launceston, the fiery daughter of ambitious Scottish settlers, she never lost her smouldering resentment at her husband's lack of drive or at her daughters' failure to make the grand marriages she had dreamt of. Her frustration vented itself in the maxims for success in life which she freely offered anyone willing, or indeed unwilling, to listen: 'Put your money in bricks and mortar'; 'Don't waste time on girls'; 'Make your pile first'. She never forgave my father for having turned my mother's head and, gripping a hot poker, she would mutter 'Cur!' when his name cropped up.

When my mother returned to office work in town, my grandmother supervised my meals including lots of tea with sugar and made me ready for school—my mother's old school, the nearby Taronga Road primary where I learned to write on a slate with a slate pencil and was introduced to a series of *Victorian Readers*.

Keats first looking into Chapman's Homer caught only a little of the excitement these *Readers* brought to me, even if at school they were under the control of crabby women with rulers. Most Victorian children of my age read these primers. Vincent Buckley detected in them a bias towards the ideology of Empire, Progress and Protestant Pluck, and perhaps he is right. But it is not a bad ideology for a child, even if there should have been more about the heroes and minstrels of Ireland and other lands than England, Scotland and Australia.

For me, in my bookless home, these *Victorian Readers* brought me to Byron and Coleridge, Mark Twain and Lafcadio Hearn and thence to Lawson, Paterson, Shaw Neilson and Roderic Quinn. Here I first learned how, in Melbourne's dusty streets, Chimborazo,

Cotopaxi and shining Popocatepetl stole W. J. Turner's soul away.

Here Adam Lindsay Gordon taught me and the whole world (or at least, the Empire) that, in the froth and bubble of life, two things stand like stone: 'Kindness in another's trouble; Courage in your own'.

To this day I can recall, word perfect, a mawkish tribute to the 'Pioneers' by a forgotten poet, Frank Hudson, and remember how my scalp tingled at his lines:

> And the swift trains fly, where the wild cat's cry
> O'er the sad bush silence broke.

The *Readers* also introduced me not only to Hans Christian Andersen and the Brothers Grimm but to Edward Lear's 'Owl and the Pussy-Cat' who danced by the light of the moon—and ate with a runcible spoon. I always recall those *Victorian Readers* with gratitude to their editors.

Those editors also had a canny habit of sticking little moral fillers at the foot of some pages. (There must be no wasted space.) They were often cryptic. A couplet from Addison, for example, noted that we mortals cannot command success and went on: 'But we'll do more, Sempronius, we'll deserve it'. I asked Carrie who on earth was Sempronius. She gave me a slice of unbuttered bread and treacle.

My mother had me baptised and confirmed in the Church of England, deeming it to be my father's church, and on Sundays she sent me to the local C. of E. Sunday school. The Bible stories fascinated me, but the school's sour-puss discipline scared me off, and a large sign on the wall which declared, under a picture of Jesus: '*Suffer* the little children . . .' seemed to me to rub it in with needless relish.

I survived whooping cough, measles and a broken arm (abruptly rebroken by the doctor a day or two later to prevent faulty setting). Above all I managed to avoid the plague of infantile paralysis and joined the shabby groups that went to gawk at children whom the plague had infected, as we wondered who would be next. Teachers at Caulfield Grammar, which I began attending in 1938, told us to avoid infection-bearing crowds, but we took little notice. It would have meant missing *Felix the Cat* or *Rin Tin Tin* or *Gunga Din* and even Guy Fawkes' Night and the Caulfield Cup, which we watched from the trees. (Anzac Day was not a problem. It held no appeal for children in Melbourne in those days. It was as sombre as Sunday school.)

Then, out of the blue, news came from my father that he was back in the money and had settled in Sydney, where he had married again. I was to join him there. He and my brother (of whom I had no memory) could hardly wait—so I was told—to see me.

The next I knew I was boarding the 'Spirit of Progress' at Spencer Street Station, in my Caulfield Grammar uniform, with a suitcase bearing a christening mug and a doctor's certificate confirming that I had not been infected with infantile paralysis.

Suddenly I felt a sort of death. I collapsed, weeping helplessly. My poor mother remarked to no one: 'That's how I bring 'em up!' To distract me, my grandfather began mimicking a heartbroken clown dragging his feet along the platform. Tears rolled into my laughing mouth as the train pulled out.

There was a tang of lager about my father when he met me in Sydney. It was a warm autumn night—Good Friday, 1939—and the holiday crowds packed Central Station. I noticed his brown eyes. He seemed both good-humoured and irritable.

'We'll go to the Show tomorrow,' he said, as he led me to a tram. 'There'll be boxing,' he said, 'dwarfs, the Mexican Rose ("the fattest woman in the world") and all sorts of freaks.'

We passed posters for *Gone with the Wind* with Clark Gable and Vivien Leigh, and for *St Martin's Lane* with Charles Laughton. 'Joe Lyons dead! Body at St Mary's!' a newsboy called. 'King Zog will fight Mussolini to the last man!'

At Circular Quay we stepped from a gang-plank on to a ferry. The harbour, dark and still, shimmered with the coloured lights of Luna Park and reflected the shadows of the Bridge—the most captivating sight of my life. At Kirribilli we walked to a flat in Holbrook Avenue—I had never known neighbours packed so closely together. I met my father's new wife, who was recovering from a mysterious operation. She accepted without warmth the responsibility for another boy. My brother showed me our bedroom and boasted he had just yanked out a tooth by tying it with string attached to a handle of a door and slamming it. He wanted me to try it. My father said no.

Do you say prayers? I asked. Yes, my brother said: 'Matthew, Mark, Luke and John! Hold the horse while I get on!'

The next morning foghorns—ghostly and alluring alarums—woke me, and my brother and I ran down to the wharf to peer across the harbour at spectral ferries and glimpse a macabre tower called Fort Denison from which each day, my brother told me, a cannon was fired at one o'clock.

Back at Holbrook Avenue we listened to the 'Daily Dozen' on 2FC and drank hot water (which did something or other for the kidneys. Like many men who drank too much, my father was a health crank.) Then we mixed Glucose-D with orange juice and took All Bran with hot milk. Tea and jam were absolutely forbidden. But there was something quite new to me—a steamed egg that they said was 'poached'.

There were many new things. Pans of stainless steel. A pot cleaner called Nigger Boy. A cleaning powder called Bon Ami. An electric jug. A refrigerator. Toilet paper (not old newspaper). Toothpaste (not soap). My father's safety razor (not long-bladed). Food I had never seen before—oysters, prawns and lobsters.

My brother took me to Neutral Bay School and initiated me into a range of new sports—Rugby Union, swimming, ice-skating at the Glaci, fishing (from the local wharf), cycling (Malvern Stars), boating, and boxing. (To urge me on, my father called me Tunner 2—in homage, I think, to his old hero, the heavyweight champion Gene Tunney.)

My brother was a sports fanatic and for the rest of his life he recalled each of these years by its cricketing drama. *This* was the year Sid Barnes was 190 not out at North Sydney. *That* was the year Ginty Lush hit four sixes and four fours in one innings. He knew Wrigley's cricket album even better than the *Lifebuoy Health Book*.

My father did not try to keep up with our sport. The years of heavy drinking were already taking their toll in ulcers and blood pressure. But he made up for it with encouragement and almost as many maxims as my grandmother: 'No son of mine sulks when he loses'; 'Never hit below the belt'; 'Never give up before the bell rings'; 'Always bite off more than you can chew and then chew like buggery'.

Only one of his saws puzzled me: 'A good billiards player is the sign of a misspent youth'. I had never seen billiards played and knew no more of the game than could be picked up from a passing glance through the swinging doors of a suburban billiards saloon—which was about as appealing as the equally seedy Penfold's plonk shop nearby. Yet my father threw a party in excitement when Walter Lindrum scored 100 in 51 seconds (and a nine-cushion cannon) at the Journalists' Club early in 1941. When I asked him why, he offered his last maxim: 'Never take any notice of anything I say'.

The nights were for me the strangest part of our Sydney life. My father was usually drunk or 'shickered', and often maudlin and defeated. 'Hughie and I will never let it happen again,' he would mumble to the walls. Hughie was some colleague from advertising and 'it' was either the war or the Depression.

He had been too young for World War I and, like so many of his age, had first been thrilled by his good luck and then regretted it for the rest of his life. In the 1930s, however, the mandatory pacifism would not let him admit it. 'I would rather see my son dead than in a soldier's uniform,' he muttered. When next morning I asked him what he meant, he was shame-faced: 'It was the booze talking'. He was delighted later with a shoddy khaki uniform he wore when he joined the Volunteer Defence Force in 1942.

As for the Depression, he blamed it for destroying the dreams of his Melbourne youth. Like his literary hero Jack London there was something of the street-corner Nietzschean socialist about him. He liked to tell us—it may even have been true—that his father had agreed to join William Lane on his utopian expedition to New Australia in Paraguay but that his mother had (sensibly) put her foot down.

'I was always a rebel,' he would say, before launching some sneers at wowsers, Catholics, Protestants, soldiers, foreigners, conservatives, imperialists, vested interests . . . All his bitterness and confusion was one day to be expressed in the novel he planned to write ('Every man has a novel in him . . .'). It was never written, or even seriously started.

He seemed happiest at his parties. Sometimes he threw several a week as if making up for lost time. Friends from advertising and journalism would drink beer and argue all night about films or books or the coming War. The films they liked were rugged, like *Only Angels Have Wings*, or socialist, like *The Stars Look Down*. But the loudest arguments were over *St Martin's Lane* and Charles Laughton's acceptance of himself. Was it manly stoicism or cowardly defeat? Someone would start a row over H. V. Evatt's *Rum Rebellion* or James Joyce's *Ulysses* or something by Ethel Mannin or Damon Runyon. One of them had written a picaresque novel in the style of Lennie Lower. Someone else had entered a painting for the Archibald Prize.

I was allowed to listen to all their banter and argument and, although I could not join in, one of my father's neighbours, a bookish and alcoholic public servant called Bert, made friends with me and chatted to me in a corner about Stalin or Hitler. He had done Classics at the university under Enoch Powell, but his main links were with the freethinkers and Trotskyists. I often had no idea what he was talking about. But whenever his rambling commentaries turned to Stalin, as they usually did, an almost homicidal rage would enliven his befuddled eyes. He later gave me my first political pamphlet—a roneoed few pages, price threepence, on the

Spanish Civil War by Leon Trotsky. (It had been roneoed on John Anderson's machine, he mumbled obscurely.) He also led me to believe that a new world war between the great powers was just around the corner and that we could have no interest whatsoever in its outcome. 'Don't let 'em fool you!' he said. I really had no idea what he was trying to say.

One day at school a strange thing happened. After we had saluted the flag, the headmaster announced that he wanted our undivided attention. He reminded us that he did not usually introduce new boys at assembly. But these new boys were different. They were foreigners. They had peculiar names. One came from Italy and one from Germany. Neither spoke much English. But, the headmaster went on, he would take a dim view (*I hope you know what I mean!*) if anyone picks on these boys just because they are aliens. We must help them in cricket and rugby and in class. We are a British country, he said, and our government has decided to give shelter to the Jews. We must show these boys what it is like to walk tall in the free-est land in all the wide, wide world.

CHAPTER 2
Messages from the Underground

The war really began for me when a grey, camouflaged ocean-liner—massive, majestic and sinister—anchored off Kurraba Point, in what seemed like my backyard. It was the *Queen Mary* of over 80 000 tons. Its job was to transport troops of the Australian Imperial Force to the Middle East. It was April 1940.

Until then the war had still seemed a faraway thing. During the school holidays, we had cheered a parade through Sydney of the first soldiers to depart. But a general revulsion against war and the leaders who had given us Passchendaele was still powerful. The yearning to believe that the war clouds meant only a dry thunderstorm ('the phoney war') was widespread, and obvious even to a schoolboy.

Australian Governments—and Oppositions—had long called for peace ('appeasement') and had even servilely removed the Digger from the great Sydney cavalcade of floats that celebrated the nation's sesquicentenary in 1938—in case it offended the Japanese or Germans. For each anti-Nazi film, such as *Confessions of a Nazi Spy* (with Edward G. Robinson), there were two anti-war films, usually French and pacifist if not defeatist, such as *Grande illusion* (Jean Gabin) or *Kermesse héroique* (Louis Jouvet). This began to change after the *Queen Mary* steamed away and France fell. During the Battle of Britain in mid-1940, my father, a son of English migrants, seemed to feel the German carpet-bombing of London or Sheffield personally.

At school we sang 'There'll always be an England' and at the annual concert draped the biggest girl in a Union Jack. One Saturday afternoon I organised the local kids into a Great Patriotic

Concert on a vacant block of land in Neutral Bay. My father had the programme printed free at the *Daily Mirror* and we raised £9 14s 1d for Alderman John Cramer's War Comforts Fund.

When Noel Coward arived in Sydney to begin a win-the-war tour of Australia at the end of 1940, hundreds of women mobbed him in the streets. This was their first contact with a legendary, embattled England and with a man whose spectacular, tear-jerking film, *Cavalcade*, was still a lively memory. Coward campaigned daily against Hitler throughout the country until he collapsed in the heat of the Queensland Christmas.

These appeals often failed. One academic pollster, an anthropologist, found many of the young to be nihilists, especially those who had recently been unemployed and still did not feel part of the official nation. Some, assuming that Britain would be defeated, asked why our troops should not stay home. Perhaps we should pull out altogether? When will Japan attack? The intellectuals—leftists, surrealists, Trotskyists, Stalinists, anarchists, freethinkers, Australia Firsters—were, almost to a man, sceptical about the war from the start. Like the generals, they were still fighting the last war. They saw this one as just another imperialist contest. (At that stage the war was still mainly between Britain and Germany. Stalin had a pact with Hitler and Roosevelt's America was neutral.)

My father had a rule of not talking about the war in front of my brother and me, at least when he was sober. If I asked him about a (Trotskyist) banner I had seen in the Domain: 'Not a Penny, Not a Gun, for the Bosses' War', or about a (Stalinist) sticker I had seen in a telephone box: 'Don't Be a Six-Bob-a-Day Butcher', he would shrug and say nothing. Often he did not know what to say—for example, when we asked him what would happen to those dangerous Nazis from the *Dunera* which was tied up in the harbour. But the house was full of newspapers and magazines and I tried to follow the talk at my father's beer parties. Our neighbour Bert also filled me in on all the dissidents, especially the surrealists and freethinkers.

As usual I did not really get the hang of it all and in any case my father disapproved. But Bert at least made the centres of resistance to the war effort seem exciting. One was the New Theatre at 36 Pitt Street (now a Japanese hotel). The Communist Party, like the Fascist Party that had some support among Italian migrants, had been banned, but it made little difference since the communists continued their agitation in the newspapers of the unions they controlled and in their various 'fronts' including the New Theatre.

For a few months from Christmas 1940 the New Theatre sponsored a witty if cold-blooded anti-war musical, *I'd Rather Be Left*. In later years few of those involved in this defeatist revue cared to be reminded of it, although one prodigal son, Jim McAuley, never denied his part in writing some of its songs.

At the time it caught the uncertainties and tensions of all those who wanted to believe that the democracies, our governments, our troops and our allies, were all doomed and absurd. Only Hitler and Stalin escaped ridicule. (The recently murdered Trotsky was not even mentioned on Stalinist premises.) Small audiences applauded, but the mainstream critics shunned the production, and its only reviews were in communist papers.

I'd Rather Be Left began as the Battle of Britain was at its height. It continued as the Sixth Division won early victories in the Western Desert and places like Bardia, Benghazi, Mersa Matruh, Sidi Barrani and Tobruk. It ran through the Battle of Greece, in which 6000 Australians were killed or taken prisoner. It ended in June 1941 when Hitler invaded Russia and the Communist Party began to support the war effort.

The musical's style drew on the combination of revue and ideology developed by Auden and Isherwood's plays at the Group Theatre in London in the 1930s. The plot was about Father Christmas, presented as anti-war draft dodger, trying to keep one step ahead of the security police. (In December 1940, security police had begun arresting anti-war activists.) In the course of the chase, lively songs spoofed politicians, journalists, warmongers and profiteers, the Australia First Movement . . . Bert had a copy of the songs and sang them for us. The retailer Sir Kidney Blow (Sir Sidney Snow) invites the politician Mr Ku Klux Klameron (the Country Party leader, Archie Cameron) to officially open an air-raid shelter:

> It is a very glorious thing
> To die for Country and King

while Father Christmas, hiding in the shelter, leads the audience (to the tune of 'There'll Always Be An England'):

> There'll always be a Menzies
> While there's a BHP
> And Menzies means as much to you
> As Menzies means to me.

(Prime Minister Menzies was in England at the time, at the height of the Blitz.)

Both 'Pig Iron' Bob (Menzies) and P. R. Stephensen's pro-Japanese Australia First Movement were the targets of another song:

> Sing *Banzai!* for Vickers.
> Hooray for Japan!
> Send all the scrap you possibly can.

(Early in the revue's run, P. R. Stephensen of the supernationalist anti-war *Publicist* congratulated the Emperor of Japan on his birthday and ended his salute: '*Banzai!*')

Jim McAuley's hand is clearest in the jazz lament:

> The rich man gets a Buick
> And gives it to his wife.
> The poor man gets a lemon
> And he can suck it all his life.

> No kiddin'.
> He can suck it all his life

and in the neutralist ditty with which Father Christmas concludes the entertainment:

> Well then, let's off to the Frozen North
> Till this stupid world gets right.
> We'll live in the snow with a radio
> And neck 'neath the Northern Light.

When the Communist Party closed down the revue in June, it replaced it with *Waiting for Lefty*.

Another of Bert's centres of disaffection with the war effort was Sherry's mid-town coffee shop at 242 Pitt Street:

> Opposite Sydney School of Arts
> assemble divers men of parts
> within a café where they sit
> baking by halves the pie of wit.

(Today the café is a Japanese pinball parlour and the School of Arts a junk shop.)

Here the bohemians—poets and artists, aesthetes and androgyns, outcastes and anarchists—would drop by to consider 'more important things' than the war. Oliver Somerville, the sour homoerotic poet, was among their number, along with the poet and art critic Harold Stewart and the poet–philosopher A. D. Hope. Harry Hooton was another: his first book of verse, *These Poets*, had been acclaimed beyond the tiny circle of poetry readers—for its gusto (by Edgar Holt in the *Daily Telegraph*) and for its urban ideology (by P. R. Stephensen in the *Publicist*). Joan Fraser looked in from time to time, and 50 years later, writing as Amy Witting, sketched some of the circle in her novel *I for Isobel*.

The bohemians did not lack material for their hatred, ridicule and contempt. They quickly dismissed the trustees of the Art Gallery of New South Wales for awarding the 1941 Archibald Prize to John Meldrum and overlooking William Dobell. With equal gusto they sneered at the coup in *Art in Australia* when the modernists supplanted the conservatives and published the first Australian manifesto of surrealism, James Gleeson's 'What is Surrealism?' (Their answer to that question was that surrealism was already dead!)

They did not waste time on the amazing new films from Hollywood (*Citizen Kane*, *The Grapes of Wrath*, *Fantasia*) or from France (*La règle du jeu*), although they identified with the gangster Jean Gabin and his suicide in *Le jour se lève*. They briskly dismissed Max Harris's poems, his new magazine *Angry Penguins*, and his championing of Franz Kafka and 'the dark forces of the unconscious'.

Oliver Somerville best captured the desperate wit of the circle. Here he is on love:

> Here, where most men are Sikes,
> I, in my secret fancy
> am Sikes' Nancy
> and look to expiate
> his muddled pent-up hate.

On Australia:

> Australia, I have heard men puffing you
> from puling platform and poetic stumps,
> this one exclaiming, 'we shall have no more slumps,'
> the other damning Japanese or Jew,
> forging our national character anew,
> feeling his own head for the abo's bumps,
> mouthing of nature's nurture—of the rumps
> of dead sheep dust-bowled over. I could spew

> gobbets like these of undigested life
> but common humanity, the world and his wife
> gloss with sublime contempt all I could say.

On life (from his 'Ballad of Bums of Times Jaded'):

> We stank of wondrous odours
> and knew not we were dead . . .

A third centre for anti-war dissidents, and Bert's spiritual home, was the Philosophy Department at Sydney University. There, while the New Theatre was rehearsing *I'd Rather Be Left*, John Anderson, the Professor of Philosophy—for some years a revolutionary critic of Stalinism and by now disenchanted with both Trotskyism and the labour movement in general—was developing his new theory of anti-politics, of permanent opposition, and of the sexual revolution.

Long influenced by Freud, he was now even more influenced by his attachment to Ruth Walker, his former student whom he had appointed to his staff. His love poems and letters acknowledge her role in the revival of his intellectual energies. ('No Pygmalion I / 'tis Galatea puts life in me.') He now saw sexual freedom as a condition of political freedom and culture, and repression or chastity as linked with political servility.

In October 1940, he presented a paper to a few friends and colleagues in which he analysed sexual slang to show up the brutal/sentimental idea of sexuality, especially the subordination of women and the macho obsession with potency. He then outlined his new theory of free and equal psycho-sexual love and its expression in what he called comic copulation—the comedy of lovers exposing the illusions of phallocentric potency. He publicised some of these ideas in lectures and articles on the work of James Joyce. He had for years championed *Ulysses* as a drama of the intellectual's struggle against Church, State, Family and all the nets that seek to restrict the growth of the free soul. Now he turned again to Joyce's play *Exiles*, which he read as a drama of free love in contest with sentimental and possessive love.

It was all too much for the conservatives. Suddenly and astonishingly, in September 1941—as Hitler's armies occupied Russia and routed the British in Africa and the Japanese army occupied Vietnam—James Joyce became the centre of a furious battle in Australia between Christians and dissident intellectuals.

At this moment when the war for the world was taking shape, Australian churchmen and their lay flocks found in James Joyce and his Sydney champion clear symbols of the malignant morality, cultural bolshevism and corrosive atheism that was threatening the world. They lobbied the tottering Menzies government, which desperately agreed to play the Christian card and ban *Ulysses*. For the intellectuals and anyone under any influence by Anderson, it was a pathetic, even contemptible act of repression. At issue was not so much a book as the future of Australia.

Hardened journalists could hardly believe their luck as, in a grim season, they found a comic, high-brow sideshow to report. Ministers of the Crown found themselves muttering about 'unadulterated filth' and circulating typed pages of 'dirty' extracts from the novel. ('Words fail me,' said one. 'My hair stood on end!' said another.) Ministers of the Cloth called public rallies to congratulate the government on its courage and foresight. Professors and writers called their own meetings to ridicule the government. The English Department at Sydney University set *Ulysses* as the theme for its Prize Essay.

So a book which few read and fewer enjoyed became a wartime symbol. Dizzy with success, the conservatives now lobbied—also successfully—for a ban on Greta Garbo's new and last romantic comedy, *Two-Faced Woman*, about a wife who poses as her vivacious, unmarried twin sister. It was, they said, an insult to decent women and wives everywhere. The ban came into effect in the week that the Japanese bombed Pearl Harbor.

The freethinkers, however, had one public triumph. Shortly

after the *Ulysses* affair, Sydney University appointed Julius Stone—an Englishman and a Jew, then working in New Zealand—to a chair of law, considering him a better applicant, by all academic tests, than a serving soldier who had been unavailable for interview. When some conservatives, and particularly servicemen, called for a postponement of any decision until after the war, the university senate at first agreed but later, after a public campaign by Anderson on academic rights, reaffirmed its original appointment. It was one of Anderson's few victories at that time but a harbinger of many more in the years to come.

One other centre of disaffection that figured in the debates at my father's parties was the Shalimar Café in the T. and G. Building in Park Street, long since demolished to become the site of a high-security U.S. consulate and an electricity authority. Here the Yabber Club and the *Publicist* push met to laugh at Britain and its Australian toadies. The name that was always mentioned was Percy Reginald Stephensen.

A Queenslander and Rhodes Scholar, he had in the late 1920s run the Mandrake Press in Bloomsbury in London and published *The Paintings of D. H. Lawrence*, *The Confessions of Aleister Crowley* and his own collection of stories, *Bushwhackers*. (D. H. Lawrence had admired his 'energy and fearlessness', but thought he lacked 'patience' and 'submission'.)

On his return to Australia in 1932, he threw himself into the publishing and promotion of Australian writers, a role for which some still fondly remember him to this day. (He was the first publisher of Patrick White—the poems collected in *The Ploughman* in 1935—and of Xavier Herbert's *Capricornia* in 1938.)

His most influential polemic was *The Foundations of Culture in Australia* (1936), which owed a great deal to Charles Maurras of *Action française*. It identified an Australian nation that was suppressed or undermined by British imperialism—as well as American materialism, Jewish and Christian universalism and cultural modernism. He demanded the 'de-Pommification and un-Yankeefying' of Australia and an end to the rule of 'bland, smug and second-rate minds'. But above all his enemy was 'the British garrison', with its control of the universities and churches and its influence over servile, anglicised Australians (the *métèques* of Charles Maurras' ideology).

This call for the decolonisation of the mind appealed to W. J. Miles, a rich eccentric of anti-British and anti-semitic disposition. Together they began a more-or-less unreadable monthly magazine, the *Publicist*, which took delight in publishing Hitler's speeches (under a heading 'Heil Hitler!'), congratulating the Emperor of Japan on his birthday ('Banzai!'), singing the praises of the *Protocols of the Elders of Zion*, attacking the Australian bourgeoisie for its treatment of the Aborigines (sponsoring a National Day of Mourning in 1938 to commemorate the beginnings of the British invasion of Australia), demanding the abolition of imperial honours (replacing them with an Order of Australia), calling for the abolition of the States (replacing them with 30 regional administrations) . . .

The more the *Publicist* was ignored, the more outrageous became its diminishing band of writers and the more odious the chat in the Yabber Club where Australians were routinely called gutless swine and our soldiers mindless mercenaries. The need for peace with Japan was taken for granted. There is no need to search for evidence of Tokyo or Berlin gold. W. J. Miles was glad to lose money on the magazine and on the whole supernationalistic enterprise. It frustrated the taxation authorities.

In October 1941, as German pilots were blitzing English cities, Stephensen formed a political grouping, the Australia First Movement, which held a few shouting matches with communists in the Adyar Hall until the police moved in to keep the peace. Someone in the Sherry's circle wrote these lines about it:

> *The Publicist* no more can please
> the ceremonious Japanese:
> its meeting in the Adyar hall

> became a most unseemly brawl,
> as Stephensen was showered with bricks
> by patriotic Bolsheviks

By December 1941, the vanities of all the centres of disaffection were thrust aside, as following its furious bombing of Hawaii, Japan conquered Burma and Malaya with a speed that challenged Germany's advance in Russia.

Scepticism about the war disappeared almost entirely. Jim McAuley reflected the new mood in his 'Ballade of Lost Phrases':

> Comrades, we argued, fought and swore;
> We might as well have stuck to beer.
> The Japanese are in Johore
> —Where are the phrases of yesteryear?

But the Japanese were soon closer than Johore as they occupied Singapore and began bombing Australia. For schoolboys, it was an exciting time, whatever their teachers or parents thought. The *Daily Telegraph* warned us that the Japanese could soon bomb Sydney and that we should forthwith close down the schools and send the children to the mountains where the various luxury and holiday hotels could be quickly converted into hostels.

Unfortunately nothing came of this good advice and we stayed home, built air-raid shelters, blacked-out the windows, boarded-up buildings, cultivated 'victory gardens' and swapped ration coupons. Almost every adult I knew either joined up or was conscripted. My father himself, despite terrible health, persuaded the Volunteer Defence Corps to take him in.

It was obvious even to me that we were in danger, although I often picked up more from my new teachers at North Sydney Boys' High than at home, since from time to time the school would assemble to honour the memory of another old boy killed and hear someone proclaim the never-convincing words: *Dulce et decorum est pro patria mori*. But my father would still not discuss the war with me. It was probably because he could find nothing optimistic to say. When sirens woke me at night, he would tell me to take no notice and go back to sleep. But even he could not conceal the fact that on the night of Sunday, 31 May 1942, Japanese submarines were shelling Sydney, although he tried to.

It became at last clear that the war was going our way when the school made the annual trip to a theatre in town to see a Shakespeare play—in 1942 it was *Macbeth*. After months of bad news—the panic-stricken flight out of Darwin, the shelling of Newcastle, the fall of Rabaul—we had won the battle of the Coral Sea, the Americans had driven the Japs out of Bougainville, the British were driving the Germans out of Africa, and the Russians were victorious at Stalingrad.

As we filed into the theatre—for a *play*! and Shakespeare at that!—the exhilarating news of the day was that Australians were advancing on Kokoda in New Guinea. It was all too much. As John Alden (playing Macbeth) turned to Doris Fitton (Lady Macbeth) and stage-whispered 'My dearest chuck!' a thousand teenagers cracked up. They cat-called, stamped their feet, shouted indecencies, tore up programmes and began punching each other. As the mêlée threatened to become a riot, the actors retreated from the stage, the management closed down the performance—and the cheers of the juvenile mob lifted the roof.

Later in the same week young vandals uprooted poplars at the Cenotaph in Martin Place. What has gone wrong with our youth? the writers of editorials wanted to know. Is it the influence of the thousands of American troops in the streets?

There was electricity in the air, a sense not only of winning the war but of a new beginning of Australian life, a surge of national pride that lasted for over 20 years. It was a period of gutsy pamphlets (Brian Penton's *Advance Australia Where?*), of nationalist films (Charles Chauvel's *Rats of Tobruk*) and plays (Douglas Stewart's *Ned Kelly* was staged) and of modernist confidence among painters (with exhibitions in New York, Washington and London).

For Jim McAuley in 'Terra Australis', the insolent emu, not the angry penguin, was the symbol of the new age: the cockatoo screams and the magpie calls you Jack, but

> . . . who shall say on what errand the insolent emu
> Walks between morning and night on the edge of the plain?

The Labor Party's spectacular victory in the election of 1943 also caught a new optimistic mood. My father took me to a packed and overflowing Sydney Town Hall in August to hear John Curtin deliver his policy speech. I had never been to anything so noisy, cheerful and belligerent. They sang 'For He's a Jolly Good Fellow', cheered the very mention of General MacArthur's name, booed Billy Hughes, and good-humouredly shouted 'Out! Out!' to the heckler who wanted to know what the hell John Curtin had done in the last war. My father clapped when Curtin promised 'No more business as usual!' in the years ahead.

But the optimists did not have the country entirely at their feet. Not all 'the phrases of yesteryear' disappeared with the fall of Singapore, and the centres of disaffection in 1941 reemerged after the crisis of 1942 had passed. The Australia First affair remained a running sore throughout the war.

When General MacArthur arrived in Canberra late in March, 1942, he shared the headlines with an extraordinary parliamentary announcement: 'Traitorous Plot Alleged. Plans for Sabotage and Assassination'. An intelligence agent in Perth had persuaded a local group of political lunatics to call themselves the West Australian branch of Stephensen's Australia First Movement and to commit to paper a fantasia of assassinations to accompany a heroes' welcome for a Japanese army of occupation.

Stephensen and 19 other members of the Australia First Movement in Sydney—who had never heard of the Perth group—were rounded up and interned. (One lived near us in Mosman—a matter for much nodding of heads and pursing of lips.) Most were soon released but Stephensen was detained until after the Japanese surrender in 1945. Writing in the official history of the war, Paul Hasluck described the affair as 'undoubtedly the grossest infringement of individual liberty made during the war and the tardiness in rectifying it was a matter of shame to the democratic institution'. He also remarked on the silence of most of the watchdogs of liberty.

Years later I met the irrepressible Stephensen. I had just published an article on the French philosopher Georges Sorel in a magazine of the Workers' Educational Association. One lunchtime, his head popped around the door of my office. 'Ah!' he exclaimed. 'Sandwiches and copy for lunch! The editor at work! As an old Sorelian myself, I want to say hello to another Sorelian!' I was as flattered that he had read my obscure article as confused at being praised by such a notorious if legendary figure.

He rattled on about Joan of Arc and Charles Maurras and then just as suddenly as he had arrived, he disappeared. I had no trouble persuading him to write his triumphalist account of his internment for the *Observer* and from then on he would pop up from time to time to chat about his disputes with Xavier Herbert or Brian Penton or Norman Lindsay. (There was no end to his disputes.) Sometimes he could be drawn on his days as a Bloomsbury publisher or his dealings with James Joyce or D. H. Lawrence or his translations of Lenin and Nietzsche. He wanted us to campaign for an independent Australian king or queen (to be selected, he said, from among the British royal family by a Regency Council of state and federal chief justices). Once he gave me a copy of his *Foundations of Culture in Australia*, which he inscribed *Rari nantes in gurgite vasto*.

The trouble was his outbursts. In the middle of literary chatter, he would let fly at 'niggers and cattle-ticks' (that is, Catholics). 'One of these days,' he might announce, 'I'll write something that will make all of you drop me entirely!' He probably had in mind some blast at the Jews. But he needn't have bothered. It was impossible to keep one's patience with him. Once, in his sitting room, I made some banal remark about the Hellenic origins of our civilisation. His lips tightened and his eyes recharged. His wife sat tight. There was a long, baffling silence. Then suddenly and grimly he spat out: 'We are not *Hellenic*. We are *Australian*!' I gave up.

When he dropped dead after receiving a standing ovation at a dinner in Sydney in 1962, I wrote an obituary which played down his fascism and played up his eulogy for the first Australian Governor-General, Sir Isaac Isaacs. It was the best I could do to acknowledge his early work. The mystery of this paradoxical man remains. The Mitchell Library in Sydney has his large and well-catalogued archive. But it does not help much. It is a sanitised archive, designed less to explain than to vindicate.

The Philosophy Department at Sydney University also soon re-emerged as a centre of opposition to the new optimism and nationalism. This was the high tide of the influence of John Anderson and his circle and it coincided paradoxically with his growing pessimism, his sense of the decline of everything he valued—from independence in public life to classical standards in education—and of the spread of everything he deplored, from planning to taxation. The alliance during the war of the democracies with Stalin and the saturation of the press with propaganda for Uncle Joe only deepened his pessimism.

This view was common enough around the world. Arthur Koestler, who had written the anti-Stalinist novel *Darkness at Noon* in a French internment camp, had summed the war up as a conflict between a half-truth (the democracies allied with Stalin) and a total lie (Hitler). George Orwell wrote that so complete was communist propaganda in England that it may be impossible to write a reliable history of these times. In Australia the propaganda was just as oppressive. We were expected to stand for Stalin in the cinemas and accept the lies of well-made films like *Mission to Moscow*.

Late in 1942 when Anderson's follower, the philosopher Perce Partridge, conducted a discussion course on politics for the Workers' Educational Association, one newspaper attacked him under the headline: 'Pro-Nazi Filth'. In a stencilled lecture, he devoted 1000 words to the question: 'Is Russia a Workers' State?' He said it was not, that the USSR did not differ significantly from fascist states and that, like them, it dealt with its critics by execution, imprisonment and lies. (In Australia, he added, the communists were limited for the moment only to lies.) The Stalinists and their fellow travellers demanded that the university sack Partridge and that people of good will boycott the WEA. No one in the press or parliament backed Partridge, although the lectures were probably the only serious critique of the Soviet dictatorship in this whole period. The university senate at least supported him.

Anderson did not limit his polemics to politics. He soon resumed his attacks on his old enemies—the churchmen who had led the assault on James Joyce and *Ulysses*. In a paper on the role of religion in education, he declared that it had no role at all, that Christian mystery-mongering, like Marxist dialectical materialism, merely engendered credulity and submissiveness and not the free spirit of inquiry.

For Anderson, to be educated is to undergo a form of conversion—from conventionalism to free thought, from dogmatism to classicism. (He was, needless to say, particularly contemptuous of the 'progressive Christianity' of churchmen like Bishop Burgmann, whose cloying charity repelled him. 'He wants to *love* me!' he complained to a friend of both men. 'I don't want his *love*!')

This time, in response to the public controversy, the Legislative Assembly modestly offered the reasonable opinion that Anderson's views were a travesty of Christianity. The university senate, relying on the same parliament's University Act, replied grandly that the university should not and did not apply religious tests.

In any case, Anderson was not deeply engaged in the controversy. There was, he said, a more serious threat to freedom—socialism, the ideology of Post-War Reconstructionism, and the planning of everything from the economy to education. The *Australasian Journal of Philosophy and Psychology*, which Anderson edited, became for a time a topical magazine and the only publication regularly repudiatiating the basic ideas of the new planners and regulators.

He delivered his main attack in October 1943 at a Philosophy Congress in a paper entitled 'The Servile State', that is, the Welfare State or the planned society. It was the major political statement of his later years. It never enjoyed the popularity of similar attacks on planning at that time by Friedrich Hayek or John Jewkes. This was only partly because of its leftist, semi-anarchist perspective. The main problem was its often esoteric, philosophic style. Sometimes Anderson had the habit of many philosophers of teasing all sorts of meanings out of obscure dicta. The fragment of Heracleitus—that a man cannot cross the same river twice—served to introduce abstruse discussions on the nature of change.

In the case of planning, Karl Marx's *Third Thesis* on Ludwig Feuerbach received, as our neighbour Bert put it, a terrible thrashing. This oracular Thesis declares: 'The materialist doctrine concerning the changing of circumstances and education forgets that circumstances are changed by men and that it is essential to educate the educator himself. This doctrine must, therefore, divide society into two parts, one being superior to society. The coincidence of the changing of circumstances and of human activity or self-changing can be conceived and rationally understood only as *revolutionary practice*.'

Anderson had used the Thesis in earlier years to attack Lenin's theory of the vanguard party, the Bolsheviks (who purport to be 'superior to society'.) It now became the basis of his attack on the other vanguard—the New Class, the regulators and planners and all those who used socialist or egalitarian ideology to advance their own interests and power.

The leftist jargon and the philosophic dialect limited Anderson's public influence in the debates on post-war planning. But his views carried weight in the universities and helped to some extent to defeat Dr H. V. Evatt's referendum in 1944 seeking power to change the Federal Constitution and introduce new controls and regulations. A small triumph in a darkening age.

But another and bigger bomb was being targeted at modernity. It exploded in the week that the newspapers were packed with epic stories of the allied invasion of France and the push to Berlin. After Hitler, the Mikado!

In Sydney, the *Sunday Sun* carried an extraordinary literary story: the first exposure of the Ern Malley hoax—in its own way almost as momentous as the front page stories. It was the first time in our history that poetry made headlines—and one of the few in the world's. It was also an irresistible drama. At the heart of it was a grim sense of two young poets in confrontation not just with the magazine *Angry Penguins* and its editor Max Harris but with great forces in the wider culture—the world's avant-garde. The stakes were high: they might succeed sensationally—or they might pay a high price for the rest of their lives. (As it turned out, they did both. They triumphed in the short term—for about 15 years—but the entrenched avant-garde have been punishing them ever since.)

After Max Harris had enthusiastically accepted the 16 obscure, modernist poems (sent to him apparently by the late poet's sister) and had published them in a special issue of *Angry Penguins* with a Sidney Nolan cover, the real authors of the poems Harold Stewart and James McAuley let it be known that they had fabricated them in one afternoon to ridicule the avant-garde. The poems, given the wonderfully meaningless title *The Darkening Ecliptic*, became the focus of a controversy that shows no sign of ending.

Stewart and McAuley knew the avant-garde from the inside. Most of McAuley's poems to this point had been obscure, modernist *cris de coeur*, which, in theme and technique, the Ern Malley poems parodied. He was also an experienced lampoonist in the university revues of the time. (In his 1941 revue, one of the hits that delighted my father's friends was a spoof of Noel Coward in Sydney. The impersonator was one Gough Whitlam.)

I had been prepared for the *Sunday Sun*'s exposure of the hoax by one of the younger teachers at school who had set a class exercise based on a review by Stewart of Max Harris's latest book of poems. The 'difficult' surrealist images are easy to invent, Stewart had written. All you do is pick any word, then look around for another completely unrelated one and stick them together. An example from Harris: 'the negro lips of Jove, pregnant and scalded with excrement'.

The teacher told us to have a go. One of us coughed up 'the styptic kookaburra' and someone else 'the broken-winded moon'. When some of Ern Malley's poems appeared in the *Sunday Sun*, my eye, trained by Stewart, immediately fixed on 'my omphagic ear' and the 'inept mountain'.

Although I was fascinated by the hoaxers' daring, the figure of Ern Malley, whose biography had been sketched (and invented) by Harold Stewart, remained a moving creation, more gripping than most of the characters I read about in Australian books. I could see him as William Dobell's 'Student', recently exhibited. There he is—the bohemian poet brooding alone in his rented room in South Melbourne. There he is again—the moody mechanic cleaning the spark plugs on a Vauxhall saloon in a garage in western Sydney. There he is once more—in the public library poring over obscure and mysterious poems. All the while he is fighting some disease, dosing himself with iodine to keep himself going, permanently irritable, refusing offers of help.

I could also see Ethel, the unhelpful but caring sister, worrying about Ern's shabby clothes, his messy table manners, his dirty fingernails as well as his poor health—the stomach pains, the loose bowels, the bad nights . . . The poems, however dim, funny or tinny, filled out the character—the dying romantic poet whose arcane gibberish is enlivened by flashes of wit and parody.

McAuley and Stewart won the first round in their contest with modernity. The impact of the hoax was overwhelming. But the modernists had time and the big battalions on their side and they could afford to wait.

Meanwhile McAuley's old friends in Sydney's modernist-anarchist bohemia took an early revenge on him for his apostasy.

They brought out *The First Boke of Fowle Ayres*, an anthology of lampoons and epigrams largely devoted to ridiculing McAuley by parodying some of his romantic verse, publishing his blasphemous anti-hymns, spoofing his interest in Christopher Brennan and guying his Byronic posturing:

> Not Looking-Glass Land's Anglo-Saxon Hare
> Could strike such poses i' the tangled air
> As McAuley, who, with his trouper's repertoire,
> Can boast a wardrobeful of attitudes,
> Who, if his gallery applaud for more,
> Will rant them vasty superior platitudes,
> And autograph their arses at the door.

My father's drinking companions enjoyed both the hoax and *Fowle Ayres*. Yet it seemed to me that Ern Malley was sometimes sitting there in their circle of lefty, modernist, egoistic and melodramatic bohemians. He would have the last laugh.

CHAPTER 3

In the Re-education Centre

Victory-in-the-Pacific Day—15 August 1945—was a dull and overcast Wednesday but nothing so trivial could stop me joining the million people who began gathering in town as soon as the radio announced the Japanese surrender, shortly after breakfast.

I went in with Bert, and we shouldered our way through the singing, dancing, laughing crowds up William Street to Kings Cross and back to the packed Domain where a radio personality conducted community singing—of everything from 'Mairzy Doats' or 'Waltzing Matilda' to 'Land of Hope and Glory' or 'Roll out the Barrel'. We bought some Atomic Crackers from a huckster shouting: 'Tickle Tojo for a tanner! Make mincemeat of the Mikado!'

'It's a funny old world, Peter,' declared Bert. I was 16 and wondered if he was already drunk.

On the ferry home Bert gave me his view of things. Peace won't last long. Maybe 20 or 25 years. The imperialists, Britain, America and Russia, are going to punish Germany and Japan just like Versailles in 1919. That will be the beginning of the next war. It's all the result of unconditional surrender. There should have been a negotiated peace. Now there will be war trials and judicial lynchings, presided over by graduates of the best law schools in America and England. The only hope is to force the imperialists to give up their empires and accept democracy. But Britain will not leave India, the Yanks will not give real freedom to the negroes, and Stalin wants a bigger empire than the Tsars and with even less freedom.

'World war by 1965. That's my tip,' Bert concluded. His kind of gloom was widespread in 1945: we were either on the road to serfdom or heading for a nuclear apocalypse. This was all too defeatist for me. Bert seemed a lost cause, one of the losers like my father, one who, also like my father, drank too much. It was some years before I began to understand them and by that time I, too, was a lost cause who drank too much.

But now I could not enter the new world fast enough. As soon as I had finished school and enrolled at the university, I left home.

It was the time of the great post-war housing shortage, but I managed to rent, for ten shillings a week, a broom cupboard or pantry in an old Phillip Street cottage, long since demolished. (The landlady said that Henry Lawson and his mother had once lived there.) My idea—partly inspired by Kylie Tennant's journalism and more distantly by George Orwell's—was to find work in places that would provide material for the novels I was going to write. I planned to be a waiter in a ritzy restaurant, a gardener in a chic villa, an attendant in a hostel for derelicts, a labourer in prison.

Reg S. Ellery's *Schizophrenia* also influenced my plans. I read it hoping—in vain—to find clues to the mysterious schizophrenic episode that had afflicted my brother for some months at this time. But I was also fascinated by the way it linked art, poetry, non-conformity and insanity with a Marxist view of capitalism that predicted a new world of mental health when we won socialism.

I quickly found a job as an attendant at the Callan Park asylum (now an arts centre) and slept at a Kent Street dosshouse and soup kitchen (now a Japanese restaurant), filling many notebooks with 'observations and reflections', to be grist to the mill of my novels when the time came . . .

My first smack of university life was when I dropped in at the SUDS (Sydney University Dramatic Society) theatre—a saloon, long since converted to more profitable uses, on the first floor of a private hotel in upper George Street—to see a rehearsal of Ernst Toller's anti-war play *No More Peace!* The producer, at this late stage growing desperate, drafted me immediately into the play.

Toller, an expressionist German poet and dramatist, was a good-hearted fellow traveller of the Communist Party who had spent some years in prison in the 1920s for his role in the Munich Soviet of 1919. As a refugee from Hitler in the mid-1930s, he enjoyed a late vogue in London before dying by his own hand in Manhattan in 1939. Edward Crankshaw translated *No More Peace!* in 1935, W. H. Auden added some political verse and London's experimentalist Gate Theatre produced it in 1936. A worthy but wooden play (far inferior to *I'd Rather Be Left*), it tells how militaristic dictators will continue to run the world until wise and decent people stop them. In 1946 in Sydney, it caught perfectly the fellow-travelling mood that saw, in the growing Western resistance to Stalin, the beginnings of a new dictatorship and a third world war.

I was cast as an army doctor instructed to pass every man, however handicapped, as fit for military service. For months, twice a week, it was my Thespian duty in our small George Street saloon to shout, among Auden's better lines:

> Halt and maimed and deaf and dumb,
> Listen to the marching drum.
> Cough or cold is no excuse,
> Narrow chest or feeble mind;
> What's the harm in being blind?
> Only dead men are no use.
> Grandad, father, mother's son,
> I will pass you all A1.

I had no problem with Toller's politics, which I more or less shared. But I had the greatest trouble throwing myself with conviction into such a stolid and pretentious play in which even I could not believe. I learnt early, in short, that I was a hopeless actor. As it happened the critics agreed with me and were harsh in their comments on my performance. It was a useful lesson and I have never trod the boards since.

But I enrolled as soon as I could in John Anderson's philosophy course at Sydney University and at the due time presented myself at the Philosophy Room to hear him address the new students.

On the the walls were crude paintings of great philosophers—Plato, Descartes, Bacon and so on. I do not how many students were turned away from philosophy by this mural *kitsch*, but at the time I ignored it. A number of *dévots* walked in, dropping their voices, pocketing pipes. Finally the Master—tall, stooped, pop-eyed, waistcoated—took up his position at the dais and began speaking in a high-pitched, Glaswegian stammer.

He took us on a *tour d'horizons*, which shocked as much as it fascinated me. Bert may have softened me up, but I was still not prepared for the full blast of Anderson's impiety. The world was going downhill fast. It was an age of socialism, religion, communism, rationalism. Abroad President Roosevelt had delivered Central Europe to communist gangsters. In Australia Labor and Liberal parties were both committed to destroying freedom and independence. The Churches and the Rationalists, the universities and newspapers, were all servile to the spirit of the times. The Ern Malley hoax, for example, was a philistine appeal to a public opinion that was worthless in matters of culture.

It was both baffling and intriguing. His manner was not histrionic and his accent was against him. But even if his answer to every question was 'No', his passion, integrity and simple seriousness stood out in a world of phoneys. His closest followers formed an exclusive sect with its own rules and rituals largely taken from the Master—stammer, stoop, pipe, beer, detective stories, bawdy songs, an open palm salute. There was also a learned dialect involving constant use of words such as 'meliorism', 'solidarism', 'voluntarism', 'relativism'. While this was both forbidding and irritating (especially if you did not like beer or detective stories), Anderson usually humanised it all with touches of personal kindness or friendship, which was rare then between the professoriate and students.

I remember in my first year standing in the winter sun in the Arts quadrangle when I felt someone brushing my arm, which had been discoloured by chalk. Turning I saw the bent tall figure and brown eyes of the great man, who went on to comment on my logic exercise. He had, he said, expected better. I was both shaken and honoured, and of course resolved to try harder. But I never became one of the family, mainly because I never took more than an amateur's interest in metaphysics.

It was in this circle that I made a friend whose companionship in a lonely period meant a good deal. It was with George Munster, who years later was an editor of the liberal fortnightly *Nation*.

Munster had arrived in Sydney just before the war among the Jewish refugees from Vienna. Now about 20, thin, stooped, chain-smoking, grinning, glancing, guffawing, he seemed to the astounded natives to have stepped from the pages of Karl Kraus' *Last Days of Mankind*. He scoffed at the philistinism of the university, smirked at John Passmore's lectures on the Vienna circle of logical positivism, and sniggered at John Anderson's disenchantment with James Joyce's *Finnegan's Wake*. He also edited a scintillating issue of the university magazine *Hermes*, which, under an epigraph from Baudelaire, introduced me to Wilhelm Reich's sexual revolution (as interpreted by Neil McInnes), to Arthur Koestler's leftist anti-Stalinism, and to a new Australian poet, a Christian expressionist called Francis Webb.

He passed on to me Hermann Broch's *The Death of Vergil*, Robert Musil's *The Man Without Qualities* and back issues of Jean-Paul Sartre's *Temps modernes*, which he found gripping and I tedious. He kept up with all the magazines—London's *Polemic*, Berlin's *Monat*, New York's *Partisan Review* or Dwight Macdonald's *Politics*. He had all the secret or rare papers or books—Wittgenstein's notebooks, Anderson's paper on sexual freedom, a typescript of A. D. Hope's *New Dunciad*, the underground *First Boke of Fowle Ayres*, the joint Arthur Koestler–Norman Haire encyclopaedia of sex, Henry Miller's *Tropic of Cancer*.

He cultivated an air of mystery—hinting with stagey Viennese bravura at irregular if not illegal deals that he had to attend to at Kings Cross or down at the wharves in Woolloomooloo. (Only a few were taken in.) His greatest qualities were his outrageous humour and his restless scholarship. At student parties, when not singing the Horst Wessel song with a Nazi salute or the Red Flag with raised clenched fist, he would stand in a corner expounding the finer points of Peter Kropotkin or Wilhelm Reich.

We all thought Munster was a genius whose furious Central European intellectuality would surely issue in a series of amazing novels, poems and discourses. They never came, although a few years later, just when the philistines were beginning to grin over another case of unfulfilled promise, he teamed up with Tom Fitzgerald to create the fortnightly *Nation*—a pale but lively homage to Karl Kraus' *Die Fackel*.

But in the late 1940s he was my best friend. When a room became vacant in his Woolloomooloo residential, I left my cupboard in Phillip Street and moved in. We would talk for hours in his haunts—Rasborsek's (for soup), Cahill's (schnitzels), Kanimbla (dumplings), Claridge's (strudel), Repin's (coffee). He didn't take to oysters or steaks, let alone pies or mulligatawny soup.

These were the last days of Sydney's bohemia, which both the Depression and the war had enriched by limiting for a few years the traditional emigration of talent. Harry Hooton was now one of its leaders. An Englishman by birth, irrepressible talker and essayist and a sort of anarchist poet, he enjoyed baiting the liberal intellectuals. In one characteristic piece of street theatre, he led a group of acolytes to a public meeting called to debate a great issue of the day—whether or not the Communist Party should be banned. A liberal professor (Perce Partridge) was making his case against all bans, when Hooton's disciples began chanting 'Down with the Fascists! Long live Art!' As the ushers tried to remove them from the hall, one leapt on to the platform, seized the microphone, glared silently at the audience, and quietly demanded: 'What is your aesthetic problem?' Others strode the aisle shouting: 'Answer his question! Long live the dictatorship of Art! Long live Aesthetics!' When the chairman was able to shout over them: 'I have called the Phillip Street police!', the anarchists retreated. 'Count them out, Harry!' one called as they left.

I went to his home for a meal one night when he was living in

IN THE RE-EDUCATION CENTRE

Rose Street, Chippendale ('the sage of Chippendale'), with his wife Thora to whom he dedicated his first book and who was now grimly on the edge of a crack-up. Harry, drunk, shouted at his son who had not done his homework.

'I am,' he confided 'a half-hearted, half-artist'. But he was more. He was a great hoaxer in the Dada tradition, with a new philosophy of Anarcho-Technocracy which some claimed to take seriously, although Harry didn't. Lex Banning, poet and wit (and victim of cerebral palsy), wrote:

> Hoot on, thou Harry, hoot!
> Bash up all the Verities,
> put in the Sophist's boot,
> while all around your rostrum
> a silly little pack
> of ignorant nonentities
> are crying quack, quack, quack.

One disenchanted Hootonite, a completely displaced person, was John Sillett. At this time he held a garage (or bed-sitter) sale of his odds and ends, mainly books by anarchists (including Hooton) whom he had come to oppose, if not despise, because of their weak-kneed compromises with bourgeois society. The only authentic human beings are lunatics and the only worthwhile discussions are in asylums. He derived all this from Andersonian distinctions: 'Is this a *quality* or *relation*?' he would demand obsessively, always seeking a pure ethical quality with no social or political relations. Munster, excited by rare books, bought several volumes by Proudhon, Kropotkin, and Bakunin. Sillett charged pennies for these valuable texts—to show his new contempt for them. I bought a copy of Harry Hooton's *These Poets* with Hooton's inscription to Noel Renouf. Sillett then vacated his little room in the city and moved into a cave.

Another of the prophets of terminal bohemia was Rosaleen Norton, a black magician or witch whose coven in Kings Cross (now a town house) was a centre for the satanic deviations celebrated in her banned paintings.

When Munster and I visited 'Roie', she showed us a few scabrous and hermaphroditic sketches and introduced us to her cats and her companion, a gentle, emaciated wraith destined for psychiatric treatment. But she was evasive when Munster questioned her about Aleister Crowley or the advice she had given Eugene Goossens for his cantata, *The Apocalypse*. She showed no inclination to initiate us into her secrets and we doubted she had any. We were wrong.

A few years later she won international notoriety when Goosens, the greatest of the composers working in Australia, was compelled to flee the country after the Press linked him with her coven. It would not happen today, but this was the high tide of dumb, post-war philistinism throughout the world. In Australia there was also something else—a lingering contest between wowsers and larrikins that did not have a real counterpart in comparable countries.

Munster and I watched some of these early post-war cases in the courts and turned up at whatever meetings of protest were called—although there were only a few in the 1940s compared with the 1930s or 1960s. The two great affairs were about ambitious novels.

One was Lawson Glassop's *We Were the Rats*, which appraised Australia and Australians in the hell of besieged Tobruk. But it distressed the Chief Secretary of New South Wales and his legal advisers because of its brothel scenes, bowdlerised stanzas from 'The Bastard from the Bush', extracts from salacious magazines and use of blasphemous words. The other novel was Robert Close's *Love Me Sailor*, about the effect of an insane nymphomaniac on the crew of a windjammer.

'Have you heard of Byron?' Glassop's barrister asked in the *We Were the Rats* case. 'No' replied the witness from the Vice Squad. 'Do you know if he was a member of Lord Mountbatten's staff for the South East Asian Command?' 'No.' 'Was he a war correspondent?' 'I'm not sure.' 'Have you heard of Shelley?' 'I know someone named Shelley.' 'Did you know Chaucer?' 'No' 'Never met him in the Vice Squad?' 'No.'

A magistrate fined the publishers £10. When they appealed to a higher court, the prosecutor was anxious to lose ('I won't press the matter too strongly, your honour. I enjoyed the book'). But the judge upheld the conviction. Everyone laughed. A few of the protesters even read *We Were the Rats*, but not many. As for the book banners, they rarely read any of the books they attacked, only selected passages.

Close had a worse time than Glassop. After the Melbourne court found him guilty of obscene libel, he was handcuffed and taken to jail, pending sentence. The Inspector-General of Prisons said:

> Officers aren't concerned with individuals. It is the normal custom to handcuff a prisoner, whether he is the author of a book or Ned Kelly. It wouldn't hurt him. He will be allowed the regulation two visitors a week and not more and you can put an exclamation mark after that. He is allowed to write nothing except a personal and domestic letter. What regulations stipulate this? I say it. I am the authority.

His sentence was a fine of £100 and three months' jail. (The publishers were fined £500.) On appeal the jail sentence was quashed and his fine increased to £150. 'Literature is not a sanctuary or an Alsatia,' said one his judges on the Full Court. These cases (and the earlier prosecution of Max Harris in Adelaide for publishing the Ern Malley poems) discredited this sort of conservatism forever. Robert Close was the last Australian novelist to be humiliated so crudely and publicly.

But in any case censorship soon became a subordinate issue. For now the Cold War—Churchill's Iron Curtain speech, the Truman Doctrine, the Rosenbergs, Fuchs, Pontecorvo and Nunn May— aroused greater passion than censorship. We began to argue far more about George Orwell or Arthur Koestler than Lawson Glassop or Robert Close.

Munster would convey, without too much precision, that he had discussed the Soviet issue with Franz Borkenau and Alexander Kerensky while they were both in Australia. His friends were sceptical, but he had one telling detail: once, seeing Kerensky in Castlereagh Street, he had called out: 'Mr Kerensky!' The Russian froze in his tracks. Turning slowly, he faced Munster and after a moment explained that the calling out of his name in public would always alarm him. The Stalinists who had murdered Trotsky in Mexico would not hesitate to kill Kerensky in Australia . . . He lived in fear.

Two books had a great influence on us. One was Lionel Trilling's *The Middle of the Journey*. We all read it as a key to the Hiss case as well as a revelation handed down about the life of intellectuals in the Cold War. Only years later did I see what cardboard figures the characters were. But at the time there was no Australian novelist even trying to pin down these familiar types: the secretly communist wife of the conforming leftist who imagines himself hounded by security police; the faithless cleric still admiring the Soviet experiment; the parasitic sponger pretending to be a proletarian; the Lawrentian bohemian babbling about Spengler; the sin-obsessed ex-communist who turns to God and denounces the Communist Party—to the disgust of his friends (except for one old-style agnostic liberal who takes a clinical interest in the 'case').

The other explosive book of these years was *The God that Failed*, a set of autobiographical statements by writers—André Gide, Arthur Koestler, Ignazio Silone—about their conversion to and disenchantment with communism. It is hard to overestimate their impact on us.

The telling point was that they all wrote as leftists, sceptical of both capitalism and communism, America and Russia. In those days it was enormously difficult for a young intellectual to desert the ambience of the left and oppose the Communist Party. But after *The God that Failed*, there was no need to be in the least apologetic for scorning the shibboleths of the traditional left. It was not only John Anderson and a few obscure Americans like Max Eastman, James Burnham or Sidney Hook who did so. It was the best and brightest of European letters. George Orwell's *Nineteen Eighty-Four* put the last nail in the coffin of conformist fellow-travelling.

These issues had already ceased to be matters for coffee shop debate by July 1947—at what the press called the Margaret Street Riot. The trigger was the Indonesian declaration of independence from the Dutch, and a widely reported insurrectionary speech by an Indonesian Trotskyist who rejoiced in the name Sourabaya Sue. Our circle supported the cause and it would also have had wider public support if some of the Indonesian leaders had not been well remembered as war-time collaborators of the Japanese.

The Communist Party called for strikes, boycotts and demonstrations against the Dutch (for whom, as war-time allies, there was a good deal of public sympathy) and leftist students at Sydney University cheerfully assembled outside the Dutch Consulate to strike a blow against imperialism.

Munster and I joined a group of observers. It seemed a relaxed occasion. Several of our friends were among the demonstrators. If we held back it was only because we felt (or wanted to feel) superior to shouting slogans and demonstrating in the streets. But suddenly burly men started punching each other. Scuffles turned into fist fights. Students were flung into the gutter and several were arrested as a crowd of hundreds (the press said thousands) packed the street to watch, boo or cheer. It was a riot.

The police claimed communists had provoked it for publicity. The communists blamed bloody-minded police thugs. The students appealed to the public for donations to pay for court actions. What had begun as a Friday afternoon diversion became a *cause célèbre*. The *Sydney Morning Herald* roundly denounced the police and called for an inquiry.

John Anderson called a meeting of his Freethought Society to denounce the whole episode. This was a tense year of the Sovietisation of Eastern and Central Europe. Stalin was advancing to global hegemony. The threat to the world does not come from the Dutch, Anderson said. It comes from the Russians. By all means criticise the New South Wales Police. But not in alliance with communist gangsters who defend the most unscrupulous police state in history. Certainly support the right of Indonesians to self-government. But Stalin is destroying the right to self-government of the Poles, the Hungarians, the Romanians and the Koreans. Margaret Street was a childish affair, he almost shouted, a communist stunt. In the 'discussion' that followed his address, the students attacked Anderson from all sides. Only Munster supported him—the same Munster who usually delighted in mocking him. It took a little courage.

The Margaret Street episode was for me a wrenching turning-point. Many of my friends, most of my prejudices and all my sense of fun were with the demonstrators. But the Cold War perspective had become irresistible.

The international tensions quickly deepened. In Russia, atomic tests. In America, the Hiss case. In Australia, the Coal Strike of 1949 and a series of communist or anti-communist rallies—in the Leichhardt Stadium, the Rushcutters Bay Stadium, the Sydney Town Hall, Balmain Town Hall, the Domain.

During the Coal Strike anything using electricity, from street lighting and trams to lifts and electric jugs, was banned or restricted. For students it was an amusing disruption of routines, even a distant intimation of social breakdown and revolution. It was also a game to take a shower in any city hotel that had its own supplies of electricty. At evening lectures we took notes by candle light and Anderson did not let slip this opportunity to note the Stalinists' encroachments on all independent ways of life, including the academic.

The closest we came to witnessing a rehearsal for revolution was during a lunchtime demonstration in King Street in August 1949, when thousands blocked the street and communist orators with banners harangued them from hotel balconies in the style of Lenin and Trotsky. If it was meant to have the makings of a revolutionary legend, it failed, but it did have the elements of an *opéra-bouffe*.

More far-reaching was the culmination of the long-standing struggle by Laurie Short, supported by the Trotskyists, Catholic Action, the Sydney press and the Labor Party, to break Ernie Thornton's communist grip on the ironworkers' union. It was a dramatic contest—the austere, slightly fanatical Short, expelled, libelled, beaten up but never beaten—against the vain, boozy, foul-mouthed but always formidable Thornton, who had built a ramshackle union into an efficient weapon in the service of Moscow. It was also a story of violence, fraud and corruption on a large scale—the Cold War in miniature.

From the tense fringes Munster and I looked on at their meetings in Leichhardt and Balmain. Years later I wanted to make a film of it all. Australian filmmakers had so often missed the great stories staring at them, and this one—Gdansk on the Parramatta River—was irresistible.

It would be *On the Waterfront* meets *Man of Iron*, with Chris Haywood or Jack Thompson as Short, Ray Barrett as Thornton. Nothing came of the idea and I don't know who would have been the director. It would probably have needed Fellini.

Then suddenly, at the end of 1949, the Second World War seemed finally over. A new deregulatory federal government was in office. Rationing was at last abolished. I had finished at Sydney University. It was a new world.

Two men rounded it off for me early in 1950—the Dean of Canterbury and Bertrand Russell. The screaming fanaticism with which mobs welcomed the Red Dean, a tall, smiling, ridiculous figure, at the Domain one wet and muddy Sunday afternoon was a new experience—as was the rowdiness the next day at Sydney University when anti-communist students counted him out.

Again John Anderson called a protest meeting—to object to the Dean's Soviet propaganda. The churchman provoked what may have been Anderson's most 'warmongering' speech. The West, he said, must drive the Russians out of Central Europe. Only the military strength of the Western powers had stopped the Russians taking over Yugoslavia or Greece. The Dean of Canterbury said he wanted peace, but peace might be worse than war—for example, a peace that meant the submission of the democracies to Stalinist misery, repression and lies.

Bertrand Russell took up this theme during his Australian tour shortly after the outbreak of the Korean War and the North Korean occupation of Seoul. However dreadful a war with the Soviet Union would be, he told us, it would be 'even more dreadful and more disastrous if the Soviet system, with all its cruelty and with all its obscurantism, were to extend over the whole world'.

During his visit to Sydney, someone had the idea of inviting him to meet a few of the philosophers at the university in what would later have been called a seminar. (The promoter, whoever it was, would not have been Anderson himself, who regarded Russell as too confused a philosopher to be worth arguing with.) We assembled in a room above the Badham Library in Science Road. Russell looked like the Mad Hatter in *Alice in Wonderland* and spoke in a high-pitched voice about perception and sense data. During the discussion he occasionally chuckled, but most of the time he looked impatient and irritated. Perhaps, someone suggested, he felt he was being transported back to Cambridge, 50 years earlier, and had to start arguing with G. E. Moore all over again.

As we filed out, I told him how much I had enjoyed his public lectures. But when I asked him whether he still urged the preemptive bombing of Russia he did not appear to hear me and looked haughtily over my shoulder.

By now I had other preoccupations. I had met Verna Scott, the only person who ever gave me a sense of life and the only person with whom I wanted to spend my days. I obscurely sensed this when we met, although it was part of the ethos of our circle not to admit to love or to regard marriage as more than a convenience.

In 1950 we decided to move to England for a year or two. We did not think about climate, living conditions, rationing or employment. Naive, provincial, nationalistic, we booked our passages as casually as moving to another State.

Once there we soon discovered why so many Australians were suffering what Peter Porter called the statutory nervous breakdown.

PART TWO

Drifting

A wandering minstrel I,
A thing of shreds and patches,
Of ballads, songs and snatches . . .
                    W. S. Gilbert

CHAPTER 4

London: 'Piccadilly Bushmen'

George Munster met us when we arrived on the boat train in London in the foggy, smoggy Christmas week of 1950. Waving the current issue of *Les temps modernes* with the final instalment of Sartre's essay on Genet and shouting that the best thing about England was its handiness to France, he soon wised us up on how to rent cheap rooms in Basement London, where to get ration coupons for the weekly egg, the chop, and the two ounces of butter, what stores accepted coupons from foreigners or Colonials, and what continental cafés served potable coffee and edible cakes. (His advice was not always reliable.)

As for warmth, in the 'hard cold English winter that breeds hard Englishmen' (as one of Job's more ridiculous comforters put it in *The Times*), you took a hot bath or popped shillings in a gas meter—the same shillings that a young suicide borrowed from his landlady for gas to kill himself with, in Peter Porter's bleak poem of the period.

In 1950 an Australian was not quite—but almost—welcomed. He did not have to bother with permits or visas, and he had the run of the country. But it was still a stodgy, grey and sullen place.

Dick Spann, the urbane Manchester liberal who later came to Sydney University, told me about a tour of the Lake District he had made about this time with the anti-socialist economist John Jewkes. They had to queue for tea in a line of drab women in head scarves and vacant soldiers in shapeless tammies.

When their turn came, a slatternly railways waitress slopped some brown liquid into their cups, spilling it into the saucers. Jewkes turned pale and seemed about to faint. Spann helped him out into the cold air. 'What's wrong? he asked. Jewkes gasped: 'It's just *like Russia*!'

It may not have been *quite* like Russia, but there was a rancour still in the air that showed itself in resentment at almost everybody—at Australians as rough, Americans as rich, foreigners as fascist, not to mention the Irish as dirty, Scots as crude, or Welsh as cheats. It was the rancour of a people who won an horrific war but now enjoyed none of the fruits of victory, the exemplary country that had lost a great empire but had not yet found a modest role. Meanwhile the newspapers were full of the Cambridge spies; Professor G. D. H. Cole wrote in the *New Statesman* that if Britain sent troops to fight China in the Korean War, he would support China; and the popular preoccupation was immigration.

'Where Shall John Go?' was the title of a series that Cyril Connolly ran in his magazine *Horizon* until it folded. My favourite was the one by Roderick Cameron about Australia:

> 'Australia? What made you go there?' he was asked.
> 'Well, I'm half Australian.'
> 'Oh! Ever been before?'
> 'No.'
> 'It's the last place I would choose to go to.'

Munster delighted in quoting Cyril Connolly's final editorial: 'It's closing time in the gardens of the West.' They were closing across the channel as well. Munster returned from a trip with the news that the great debate among French intellectuals was what to do when the Russians moved in. Would they cooperate with the Reds as readily as they had with the Nazis? He thought they would be even more cooperative and told everyone to read Arthur Koestler's new novel, *The Age of Longing*, about the coming fall of Paris to the Russian Army.

As soon as we could we crossed to Paris ('While there's still time . . .') where Munster showed us the sights. That's the café, he told us, where Simone de Beauvoir wrote *Le deuxième sexe*. Over there was the very spot where Koestler tossed a glass of water over Sartre. This was where Camus sat.

We watched massive demonstrations against the United States as Wilfred Burchett's spectacular stories of American germ warfare in Korea became Australia's major contribution to the history of war propaganda. I discovered, and became the lifelong student of the critic Raymond Aron, and we followed the bitter debate between Camus and Sartre over Stalinism.

But however intriguing Paris was as a city, French intellectual life was in a low period, dominated by fellow-travelling clichés. The editor of the new bulletin *Preuves* told me, with a Swiss objectivity, that the French were 'morbid' and he was right. Their role in the war had been ignoble and they still resented the Allies, especially the Americans, for winning it and deciding the fate of the world without the benefit of French advice. Whatever its faults, London was a livelier centre—and was changing for the better all the time.

Kingsley Amis, Philip Larkin and Kenneth Tynan were preparing their assault on the stodge-masters of English literature, stage and academia. The 'Movement' poets were beginning to supplant the older surrealists (the English Ern Malleys). The director Alexander Mackendrick made the stunning film *The Man in the White Suit* (starring Alec Guinness), a black comedy which confronted a society that had lost integrity, enterprise and humanity. Malcolm Muggeridge became editor of *Punch* and brought a new wit to London journalism. It may not have been the New Elizabethan Age of the public relations industry but it had its moments of excitement.

One such moment for me was a wet Tuesday afternoon in March 1951 when Michael Oakeshott, the 'anti-conservative conservative', delivered his inaugural professorial address in the dun citadel of socialism, the London School of Economics.

It turned out to be a symbolic occasion. Hundreds of students, graduates and visitors, including scores of Africans and Indians, packed the main hall and crowded the overflow rooms and corridors that had been fitted out with a public address system. Everyone felt that Oakeshott, the Tory wit and student of St Augustine, David Hume and Thomas Hobbes, would exorcise the ghost of his predecessor, the leftist Harold Laski.

Suddenly the crowd, the School and Houghton Street itself fell silent. You could have heard a pin drop, as Oakeshott, lean, handsome, good-humoured, entered the hall . . . The microphones clicked on and his insinuating and occasionally acidulous voice reverberated through the building. We all strained to catch his slow opening references to Laski:

> It seems but an hour ago that he was dazzling us with the range and readiness of his learning, winning our sympathy by the fearlessness of his advocacy, endearing himself . . .

and so on. Then more slowly and sonorously still, as if reading a poem: 'and it seems perhaps a little ungrateful that he should be followed by a sceptic, one who would do better if he only knew how'.

The lecture then settled down to a critique of ideological politics. It was a compelling mixture of scepticism and commitment, conservatism and bohemianism, traditionalism and eccentricity. I immediately decided to attend his lectures. When I met Oakeshott I was struck by both his enjoyment of life and a barely masked rage towards frauds. But I was always grateful to him for introducing me to an English style of thought that brought me closer to 'what all those wars and poems are about'. (When I asked him years later why he had never visited Australia where his voice was badly needed, he said: 'Nobody has ever asked me'.)

The emerging confidence in England also showed in the partly ridiculous, partly exhilarating Coronation of Queen Elizabeth. After all the ballyhoo in the press about the New Elizabethan Age, I had assumed the Coronation would be another sham. It was in fact an authentic popular celebration that made—this was the only comparison that came to mind—the Victory over Japan holiday in Sydney in 1945 seem tame. It was as much a nationalist as a royalist occasion, a celebration of British exceptionalism.

The world at large had abandoned its traditional rulers and institutions, its kings and queens, and for a moment had sung its hallelujahs to sundry Hitlers and Lenins, while Britain remained free, democratic and monarchist. Now, with prosperity at last returning, and the controllers and regulators in retreat, the British were in a mood to celebrate.

But they were not celebrating Tory traditions. Barely were the Coronation celebrations over than Swinging England began its great assault on British traditions. Nor were they celebrating the Empire. They could not abandon it quickly enough. Scotland played an official role in the Coronation ceremony in Westminster Abbey, but there was no place for Australia or Canada.

Such considerations, however, were lost in the general euphoria. During the parade after the ceremony, I stood, by chance, in Oxford Street where a set of carriages bearing imperial leaders stopped for a few moments. Mr Holland of New Zealand, unable to restrain himself, jumped up and down like a jack-in-the-box waving at the crowd and shouting Maori greetings. The Queen of Tonga also waved indulgently. Mr Nehru, with a better grasp of the facts, stared moodily at us from his carriage, and finally yawned mightily—at me, so it seemed.

But English enthusiasm, especially in the street parties, was almost universal. (Low's famous cartoon deploring the waste of it all showed a dour lack of imagination. As Malcolm Muggeridge once put it to me: Low had a magnificent line but a commonplace mind.)

The republican editor of the *New Statesman*, Kingsley Martin, breezily dismissed republicanism from the British agenda, and even Muggeridge brought out a special and thoroughly royalist issue of *Punch*. If *Punch*'s monarchism was among the reasons why he always said he did not enjoy his stint on the magazine, there was no sign of it in 1953. But it was only a matter of months before he wrote the first of his cautionary lampoons of royal soap operas, before John Osborne described the Royal Family as the gold tooth in a mouthful of decay and the crowds began flocking to the Royal Court to see *Look Back in Anger*.

About this time Oakeshott mentioned a proposal to start an English link in an international network to defend cultural freedom against Stalin and the Soviet expansion. I didn't realise it was the birth pangs of the magazine *Encounter*. He referred to a group of eccentrics, including Malcolm Muggeridge, who was, he said, obviously in charge, and Bernard Wall, who wore big boots and was always talking about Italy. The trouble was their continuing argument about the policy of the famous magazine *Nineteenth Century and After*, which had been formed some 80 years earlier and had in its time published all the famous British writers from Gladstone to Oscar Wilde.

The two old ladies who owned it sold it to the Congress for Cultural Freedom in Paris, which changed its name to *Twentieth Century* and started to publish all sorts of Continental and American anti-communists from Franz Borkenau to Irving Kristol. But it did not catch on in England.

A literary faction led by Stephen Spender wanted to revive the *Horizon* tradition, but the political toughies thought that poetry and art were for pansies and that England badly needed more philosophy to make people think, and more politics to wake them up about Stalin. Oakeshott's idea was that the magazine should become the sort of thing that Karl Kraus would have wanted to edit. But in the end a compromise was struck between Bloomsbury and the hard-liners. *Encounter* was launched in 1953, edited by Stephen Spender representing Bloomsbury, and Irving Kristol from New York representing the toughies.

Some time later I asked Kristol what it had been like for a young American—he was barely 30—to start a major new magazine in London. He said in his cut-and-dried way: 'It was easy'. He added: 'There was nothing to read in London then'. He meant that the great English periodicals had all folded—

Cambridge Journal, Scrutiny, Horizon, Penguin New Writing. But he conceded: 'You had to be a screwball, like Cyril Connolly'. He had not been prepared for two English phenomena. One, which he had to accept, was the strength of the homosexual cult in the English literary world. ('It was unthinkable at that time in Jewish New York.') The other, which he had to combat, was the philistine anti-Americanism or universal anti-anti-communism of the intellectuals. The *Times Literary Supplement* condemned his first issue of *Encounter* for its 'negative' anti-communism. 'Did anyone ever attack us during the war for "negative" anti-fascism?'

The magazine lasted about 35 years, keeping the Cold War before a public which often wanted to close its eyes. It also kept one foot in the Bloomsbury camp and tried to restrain the modish anti-Americanism. It aimed to be an English magazine, not too international or cosmopolitan. Yet T. S. Eliot, a legendary editor as well as poet, refused to write for it because he saw it as an organ of American propaganda. Despite its great achievement, its disappearance in 1990 was only perfunctorily mourned.

But it had a difficult charter. The Paris office of the Congress for Cultural Freedom and American readers always wanted more politics and more exposures of morbid anti-Americanism. The English supporters however wanted more literature. For a time the English hands—especially Muggeridge and Spender—wanted to replace Kristol with the more anarchistic Dwight Macdonald, but the idea fizzled out.

Under all its pressures it is amazing that it published so much that was so good. The French critic Raymond Aron always regarded it as the best thing published in the English language and I for one agreed. It was out of its example that *Quadrant* emerged.

But the issue that tortured or at least preoccupied Australians in London was entirely different from all this. It was the great question: Are you going to stay on and become an expatriate (with undertones of desertion but the hope of achievement)? Or are you going back (with undertones of provincial irrelevance but the sense of working with and for your own people)? It was the old and continuing question: Do you follow Frederic Manning, W. J. Turner and Henry Handel Richardson . . . or Henry Lawson, Miles Franklin and A. D. Hope? Jack Lindsay or P. R. Stephensen? Peter Porter or Les Murray?

It is extraordinary how much passion and sometimes bitterness went into this choice. It was not always a matter of long arguments, although there were some. Often a word, a nod, or a question spoke volumes. A casual remark by Ken Minogue to David Armstrong, or Jill Neville to Roger Covell, or Murray Sayle to Milo Dunphy might be pondered for months.

Patricia Rolfe in her neglected novel *No Love Lost* caught some of the deformations of character fostered by London life. One is the talentless expatriate from pre-war days who lets the heroine think he was one of the Auden–Isherwood circle and had fought in Spain. ('Did you ever actually meet Hemingway?') There is also a grubby poet pretending to be a homosexual and the professional Aussie expatriate who burns gumleaves at parties (and burns herself to death). They all have in common a consciousness of failure and a face-saving determination to remain in London—'in the centre of things'.

Barry Humphries caught the other deformations—of those who were 'going home': Buster Thompson, the affluent lout pub-crawling his way through his Western heritage ('Copenhagen takes some beating, all that lovely ice-cold Carlsberg'). Debbie Thwaite is his female counterpart. ('Mind you, I must admit there are compensations for living in London. For instance, cheese is cheaper.') Back in Australia the Minister for National Identity sketches his plans for a universal and mandatory Australian style: an ultraviolet suntan regulated by subcutaneous injections and a compulsory nasal twang enforced by immobilising the tongue with an Ausmophone fitted to the throat.

But the major dramatic treatment of the theme was Ray Lawler's bitter play, *The Piccadilly Bushman*. It is about an Australian actor (played by Guy Doleman) who has made a successful film career in London and has come to despise his native land, the friends of his youth, even his wife, now a drunk drab. Ridiculing Australians has become one of his better party turns in London, although they still provide him with a means of income: the play begins with his return to Sydney to make a film based on an Australian novel, or on its distortion for the international market.

But as the play develops, the heartless, opportunistic actor becomes the real hero of the drama. His art has mandated his life abroad as much as it did, say, Melba's or Sutherland's. It is a secretion of the blood (as Martin Boyd put it). A 'hundred generations' have pulled him to Europe. Yet he knows he must pay a price: he can never accept his own country and England will never accept him. He is a despised and self-despising expatriate!

The play offers no solution. There is none and the argument smoulders on. In his play *Emerald City*, David Williamson contrasted the idealistic national dramatist who can only write about his countrymen, with a squalid internationalist hustler. In an essay, 'An Expatriate's Reaction to His Condition', Peter Porter threatened that the next time someone dismisses him as 'the expatriate poet', he will dub Les Murray 'the *patriot* poet'.

In an open letter, the stay-at-home dramatist Barry Oakley wrote to his friend the novelist Desmond O'Grady, who has made his career in Rome: 'By staying home, I too have travelled . . .'

For my part the gusts of argument gave way to more personal events. My father died about this time. I was more devastated than I had ever been since my mother's farewell on Spencer Street station before the war. Yet how little time I had ever spent with him or under his roof. The strange thing was that we had come together in our letters to each other, while I was in London. The poor man's bluff and baffled love—he knew he was dying, although I did not—still brings tears to my eyes. I no longer despise his limitations, having become far more aware of my own.

My life now was tied to Verna. After the death wishes, the drunkenness, the 'statutory breakdown', I knew that I would find some point in life with her or not at all. I bought a ring in Regent

Street. A friend from Sydney came along as a witness and we were married in a now defunct if not demolished Registry of Marriages on a hill of a now defaced Hampstead. It was a wet, wonderful spring day which remains for me the London of my dreams.

CHAPTER 5

Khartoum: 'Only connect...'

But where to go next? We weren't ready to return home, even if we could have found the fares. It was all very well for Munster to mutter, as he did once after a funeral—I think it was Norman Haire's at the East Finchley crematorium: 'The goat must graze, as Proudhon said, where it is tethered . . .' This goat was not tethered to England and still had itchy feet.

Thumbing through the overseas appointments columns of the *Times Educational Supplement*, you would find offers of passage to outposts of Empire where you were paid generous, tax-free salaries to help lay the foundations of decolonisation and self-government. The offers usually included an 'outfit allowance'— tempting to a vagabond emigré who could do with a new suit. There were posts on offer in Sierra Leone, where you could pretend to be Graham Greene among the cockroaches. Or Zanzibar where Evelyn Waugh, his head soaking with eau-de-quinine, inquired about voodoo . . .

One spring morning in 1954, we stumbled on an advertisement by the Government of Sudan—the land of the Mahdi, General Gordon, and the New South Wales Contingent commemorated on a plaque near the old Fort Macquarie, now the Opera House. By 1954, Sudan was being 'Sudanised', that is, the British officers who ran the army and police, the district commissions and civil service, were being 'retired' and replaced by Sudanese. The Sudan Government wanted school teachers on short contracts. There would be no more 20-year contracts with no leave for seven years.

I wrote to Sudan House and matters moved with amazing speed. I was summoned to St James's for a quick interview with

Sudanese and English officials, one of whom confided: 'Don't miss the Temple of Queen Hatshepsut before the Egyptians flood it'.

Next the consulting physician examined me briefly, and gave me a tip: 'Kill the hyenas. Quick and lively. They're chock-a-block with rabies. Jackals too.' Then someone gave me the *Sudan Almanac* and sent me off to Golden Square for tropical clobber—light, loose suits, shorts and shirts, cummerbund, mosquito net. The outfitter recommended a hat ('At Ramadan, Khartoum reaches 110 degrees') but I refused. The *Sudan Almanac* was full of advice: 'There is no virtue in excessive alcohol' for the treatment of scorpion stings. If you pick up lice, dust yourself with DDT. Don't keep goats: their milk may give you Malta Fever. Never buy a second-hand *angareeb*. Don't shoot game from a moving vehicle (except crocodiles). Be careful where you swim: you get bilharziasis in stagnant water. Visit the latrine at the same time each day. If your urine is black or red, you have Blackwater Fever and should stop taking quinine immediately. Keep the lepers in huts 20 yards from the village. Don't shoot a rabid dog in the head; tie it up and leave it to die, then send its brain, cut into halves, to the research laboratories in Khartoum. In the *nigma* season, burn dung fires at night on the windward side of your stables, but if your horse still picks up African Sickness, burn the carcase. (Your mules should survive if rested.)

In no time we were aboard planes to Khartoum. It was as if one minute we were queuing in the snow outside the Everyman in Hampstead to see a Cocteau film, and the next we were strolling through the dusty streets of Khartoum—with its coughing donkeys, gargling goats, barking camels, and the scent of jasmine mingling with the stench of a camel-drawn night-cart or with the blue exhaust fumes of the ubiquitous Ford Consul.

At the Grand Hotel a fat, surly waiter in a green cummerbund responded to the clapping hands or snapping fingers of Germans, Americans, Armenians, Egyptians—the motley itinerants roaming Africa for any pickings to be had from decolonisation. But who was I to be snooty about it? Was I not one of them?

'Won't pay their bills. Wrong types,' someone said.
'Full of gin. She sweated so much you couldn't hold her. Naked.'
'Makes it harder for the rest of us.'
'They were up in the trees not long ago.'
'You could see his bints coming and going every night.'
'He shouted at the poor bloody cook to corner her. One eye on Allah and one on memsahib.'
'He said "Lock me up or I'll shoot her". Didn't trust himself.'
'You have to grease their palms all the time.'
'She could never face the servants again. Sent her home.'
'Never come across a race so interested in money.'

A boy in a white *jellebeya* with a fly swatter hanging from his neck dragged his feet across the floor and, from time to time, rang a bicycle bell while almost holding up a blackboard with my name on it. The hotel clerk, who wore polaroid glasses indoors, had our tickets to Wad Medani, the great cotton centre near the school to which I had been posted.

The English headmaster and his wife met us at the Wad Medani airstrip and drove us past fields of cotton and lines of African cotton-pickers resting under euclayptus trees, past a *suk* with swarms of flies, past a Greek general store with a shaded veranda, past the club surrounded with barbed wire and the open-air cinema, down to a ferry which took us across the Blue Nile to a jetty near our bungalow. A crocodile peered at us lazily.

The English couple—athletic, honourable and good-humoured—wanted to see through the transition to self-government and hand over a good English school to the new rulers. Fear of the future, let alone despair, was entirely against their principles and they were loath to admit that their life's work would not endure in the new Sudan—with its tribal and racial enmities, windy rhetoric, fanatical leaders, venal politicians, cynical expatriates, and Americans determined to clean up the mess.

At dinner that night—an operatic affair in a scented garden under a glittering sky—the other teachers were more alcoholic and talkative. Sudanese students, they told us, were a queer lot. Fond of Hitler. Down on Negroes and Jews. And Egyptian women.

Not too keen on the materialism of the oil sheikhs. Or so they say. No time for King Farouk, most of them. But they love big words like brotherhood. The Americans encourage them. The other day one of the Americans was amazed that the English-speaking Africans and French-speakers don't talk to each other!

'Uncle Sam will fix all that! Then the Russians will be next. Forget about the *Almanac*. Get in plenty of Andrew's Liver Salts. Good for hang-overs.'

We were after all agents of decolonisation in the new age of Bandung—the now forgotten era when President Sukarno first proclaimed the fall of the West and the rise of the Third World. If we heard Radio Cairo denouncing us as imperialists and racists and exposing the Church of England minister as a spy, or the Sudanese leaders proclaiming how the British vultures and mad-dogs had stolen the great wealth of Sudan, we were to remember E. M. Forster's 'Only connect . . .'—and the Andrew's Liver Salts.

I had an early lesson at the Wad Medani Club—an English club in the St James's style, with dining room, library, card room and pool—when the Prime Minister gave us a talk on the Bandung Conference which he had attended with Gamal Abdul Nasser of Egypt. How impressed he had been, he told us, with Dr Sukarno's proclamation of the end of the age of the predatory white man and the rise of the new multi-racial, multi-religious world order! We must mobilise, he had said, *the moral violence* of Asia and Africa in support of peace and tolerance.

No-one believed a word of this humbug but when I tentatively asked the Prime Minister about the reports of massacres of blacks in southern Sudan, he smiled and looked disdainfully into the distance. 'And how are things in White Australia?' he finally asked.

The school day began at 6.30 a.m. with a long break around noon when the British took shelter from the sun. (Sitting in the bath under the fan with a long gin and tonic was recommended.) The students quickly tested me with barely restrained scorn for the materialist and Christian West. (The only Westerners they admired were Abraham Lincoln, Hitler and Stalin.)

It was easy to control my irritation. My own prejudices were after all not so distant from theirs. My problem was to reach—and teach—them through an English curriculum that they saw as the absurd burden to be endured for the sake of qualifications. Without an English school certificate, no student would have a chance of becoming a civil servant with a small moustache. Otherwise the English course simply bored them.

Hamlet was the Shakespeare text for the year. The Licos cinema across the Blue Nile agreed to have a special showing for us of Laurence Olivier's film (which I had ridiculed with such ignorant zest at Sydney University). It was not a good idea. It angered the students. Hamlet, they told me, was clearly a man of low character. Why? Because *he had been so rude to his mother*. She too was clearly a good woman, since she wore a long dress, unlike the unspeakable Egyptian and English women.

They responded to the themes of assassination, coups, spying, exile and revenge, but they still insisted that their government should not have allowed the impious Hamlet–Gertrude scenes to be exhibited in a Muslim country. We might have done better if we had not gone to the film.

I was able to reach some of the students through another text in our curriculum—Joseph Conrad's *Gaspar Ruiz*, a gothic tale of love and death in the revolutionary wars of South America. Luckily it had not been made into a film. Its climax comes when Gaspar Ruiz, the heroic peasant leader of Indian guerillas, uses his massive back as a gun carriage for his cannon, in an attempt to rescue his Castilian wife from the republican insurgents. The ordeal kills him. His wife hurls herself to death in a ravine. Their surviving daughter inherits her father's strength, her mother's eyes.

Conrad's dark story, with its violence and sacrifice, treachery and despair, loyalty and physical strength spoke far more directly to the new generations of Africa at the beginning of the age of revolutionary nationalism, negritude and pan-Arabism than E. M. Forster could. We would never *connect* on the level of ideology and politics, but we could reach each other in a tale of simple tragedy.

But even this was confusing. One night a group of striking students marched around the school in a protest against Abyssinian persecution of Muslims in Eritrea. An old sheikh who gave religious instruction told us the students were acting under instructions from Prague. In any case they were exalted. 'It's just like Gaspar Ruiz,' one said darkly, as I stood watching them against an orange, pink and blue sunset over the Nile. 'We *must* spill blood,' said another prophetically, 'if we are to create a new life.'

One group that felt left out of the new life was the black Christian minority. The Christians usually fell silent as the Arabs celebrated the great days to come. One night the whole school went to the cinema to see Mervyn Le Roy's *Quo Vadis*, a Hollywood saga of Nero's war with the Christians, starring Peter Ustinov as Nero and Robert Taylor as the Roman commander who falls in love with a Christian girl, Deborah Kerr. For some years the British administration had banned the film as offensive to Islam, but under the transition government it had slipped through the censorship. Perhaps the new Muslim authorities thought its vulgarity would damage the Christian cause. Yet the poster that advertised it was the only announcement pinned on the local Church of England notice board.

In any case the cinema was packed—the British in their white shorts with whisky flasks in the balconies, the Sudanese in *jellebeyas* in the back stalls, and the black Christians in shorts and singlets in the front stalls. The main film would not begin until about 9 p.m.—in the cool of the evening. Until then we endured a torrid Egyptian domestic drama with plenty of belly-dancing and screaming. The front stalls began to grow restive and the British clapped for more soda to make the whisky go further.

Finally the Christian epic began. Its great moment came when the Christian slave, Ursus, alone and unarmed but a true believer, confronts an enraged bull in a Roman amphitheatre and slays it with his bare hands. At this triumph of Christianity over its persecutors, the Africans in the front stalls stood on their seats, cheered, yelled and shook their fists. The Arabs in the back stalls looked around for the police. The British wondered how long it would take to run to the club. When a drunk Christian attacked an Arab with an axe everyone disapppeared into the night.

I began reading General Gordon's Khartoum diaries at this time—one of the few irresistible books in the club library. By the end of the Mahdi's siege of Khartoum, Gordon, facing death, now believed that the fundamentalist Arabs were superior to the liberal English. The cracked hero recognised himself in the Mahdi and preferred to die among the Arabs than to live in modern Britain. Gordon's shadow still lies over the Sudan—although not as long as the Mahdi's.

It also lay over a novel I wrote at this time. It was a bad novel, never accepted for publication, and full of awkward dialogue, big thoughts and the influence of all sorts of novelists from D. H. Lawrence to Saul Bellow. But it was my little *summa* for the moment. I called it *When Light Rode High* from Shelley's lines:

> When light rode high, and the dew was gone,
> And noon lay heavy on flower and tree.

The idea was the light of reality succeeding the dew of illusion. The characters included a freethinker on the edge of his 'statutory breakdown', a Dostoyevskyan revolutionary, an urbane conservative at ease with the world, and a tortured Christian very ill at ease (with a touch of General Gordon). At the centre of the action is, of course, an artist! There is little development and much turgid argument. But in the end, in a rage of self-hatred, I let baboons tear the freethinker to pieces somewhere in Africa and the artist burns all his paintings.

I had plainly reached another dead end. But we were at least half way home. When my contract ran out, we took the train to Port Sudan on the Red Sea to wait for a ship to Sydney.

As one last African exercise, I set out to find the obelisk erected by the imperial government to acknowledge the more-or-less useless contribution made in 1885 by an imperialist New South Wales Government to an avenging if abortive reoccupation of Sudan after the Mahdi's slaughter of General Gordon in his palace in Khartoum. The New South Wales Contingent of some 770 men (with 218 horses) was the first Australian expeditionary force to engage in an imperial war.

They were stationed outside the ancient but now abandoned port of Suakin, some 40 miles south of the modern Port Sudan. For a few weeks in temperatures of 115 degrees they began laying a railway line to Berber, on the way to Khartoum. It was more a gesture of psychological warfare than an engineering project. They did not lay much line and they did almost no fighting. Six died of dysentery and fever before the rest were packed off home and the British Government forgot about Sudan for several years.

They also forgot about the New South Wales Contingent, which at the time had been more a nuisance than a help. But 14 years later there was a Boer War, in which Australian troops would certainly be welcome. Lord Kitchener remembered the earlier expeditionary force and put up an obelisk to honour it. A policeman told me that he half-remembered seeing it as a boy but the desert winds must have blown it away long ago, and who cares? He was right. The British presence in Sudan was passing and would soon be forgotten entirely. Years later I mentioned this lost obelisk to the minister responsible for war graves and memorials, but he urged me to forget all about it. General Gordon would have agreed.

As we kicked through the sand dunes, we heard a distant muezzin call the faithful to prayer from the minaret of a mosque in the centre of empty streets of the abandoned town. We gave up searching for the Australian obelisk and boarded a Swedish cargo ship for home.

CHAPTER 6

Canberra: Looking for a Life-belt

In Sydney's Lower George Street—it was 217A, now the site of a great Japanese hotel—there was a small shop with some narrow stairs beside it. They led us up into a large, drab room where we were welcomed by a fragile, diaphanous lady in white who bore the marvellous name of Imogen Whyse. It was the Poetry Society and she was its moving spirit.

The occasion was the first public reading by James McAuley of his new satire on Australian life, 'A Letter to John Dryden'. A number of poets was standing around in the packed room. Near the door was Charles Higham, pale, underweight and shock-haired. In the middle was A. D. Hope, abstracted, disdainful, prophetic. Across the room was Jim McAuley himself, looking like a Spanish painting by Zurbaran.

Imogen Whyse, in her most literary and affected manner, introduced McAuley to Higham—'one of our discoveries'. The meeting was, Higham told me later, among the important events of his life. 'We hardly spoke but McAuley's penetrating eyes gazed into mine and saw an artist. I had found a brother in the dark night of Australian philistinism.'

There were other less likely poetry lovers there—Hal Wootten, later famous as a Royal Commissioner on Black Deaths in Custody but then fresh from anti-communist triumphs in the courts. With him was John Kerr, QC, later famous for many things but then resisting McAuley's blandishments to lead something to be called the Democratic Labor Party.

McAuley spoke briefly about his more-or-less traditionalist poetics. ('Poetry ought to be intelligible at its first reading aloud.')

His doctrines were in any case well known to the members of the Poetry Society where he had often discussed them—the society being his main literary base before he became founding editor of *Quadrant*. He laughed at 'the boarding house hash' of most Australian poetry, that is, its confusing of poetic styles, and spoke up again for 'occasional poetry'—written for public occasions, such as his 'Prologue' for the opening of the Elizabethan Theatre in Sydney or his 'Royal Fireworks' for the Queen's visit in 1954: 'Poetry is not spun out of your navel in an ivory tower'.

He then read a number of his new poems, including one about Mozart's *Magic Flute* in which he took Pamina's 'All is lost' as her lament for the almost forgotten civilisation of pre-modern Europe. But the high point of the evening was his reading of his *A Letter to John Dryden*. He begins by noting how hard it has become to catch the interest of this 'vacant, sly, neurotic modern world', especially now that the schools and universities have made sure that there is:

> No fear at all the student will find out
> What all those wars and poems are about.

He then examines and rejects three creeds competing for the allegiance of modern man—revolution, tradition and liberalism. Finally he turns to Christ. But how to convince a people who reject Christ and for whom 'good and evil are but culture traits'?

In a magnificent conclusion McAuley appeals for prayer:

> Incarnate Word, in whom all nature lives,
> Cast flame upon the earth: raise up contemplatives
> Among us, men who walk within the fire
> Of ceaseless prayer, impetuous desire.
> Set pools of silence in this thirsty land.

It was an unforgettable night, my first intimation of a deeply felt critique of Australian secular liberalism wrought by an Australian writer out of Australian experience. The satire provoked its counter-satires—by Jack Lindsay ('Unsolicited Reply'), Amy Witting ('A Letter to James McAuley') and A. D. Hope ('Lambkin: A Fable'). But it remains the greatest of our satires.

McAuley was already acting editor of the as yet unpublished and still unnamed literary quarterly which finally became *Quadrant*. He told me it had an office in Albert Street—in that precinct around the Quay that had long been the centre for the arts—Bryant's Playhouse, the New Theatre, Buggery Barn, the Society of Realist Art, the Poetry Society, the Fellowship of Australian Writers, all since expelled for tourist hotels or office blocks. But the magazine had no money beyond a small subsidy of £200 a month from the Congress for Cultural Freedom in Paris (they had budgeted for £945 a month) and, although he hoped for some Commonwealth Literary Fund support, he was not optimistic.

For his part he had not yet been formally appointed editor, and there were those, he knew, who simply could not accept the idea of their editor being a Catholic, and a convert at that (although McAuley said he preferred to be called a revert, since he had reverted to the faith of his father's family). He was in fact confirmed as editor soon after the Poetry Society meeting.

We agreed to talk more about the magazine, although this was more a hope than a plan since I almost immediately left Sydney again—to go to Canberra where Perce Partridge had invited me to join him at the pallidly named Australian National University, with my old friend Eugene Kamenka and teacher John Passmore. I had no other job and Verna was expecting our first child. I accepted the offer gladly. But McAuley's invitation echoed in my mind.

The Australian National University had only recently been established and everyone had a different idea of what it was all about. For 'Panzee' Wright of Melbourne, it had grown out of his war-time discussions in Colonel Alf Conlon's 'small back rooms' about what would happen to Australia and to civilisation if Western Europe were destroyed. (It was the age of catastrophism.) Why should not Australia be a new Constantinople? Let us create a great university—a new All Souls or Princeton—and attract back to Australia all the famous but expatriated scientists and humanists—the sort of scholars who, from the days of Gilbert Murray or Samuel Alexander, had been obliged to make their careers in the metropolitan centres abroad.

Others of more mundane or commonsense disposition saw the new university simply as mobilising an academic elite to do work of particular significance to Australia—from the development of nuclear power to our relations with Asia or the South Pacific. The wan name and its acronym, ANU, suited their purposes well. In any case it was perhaps the last of the major manifestations of post-war nationalism—the sort of official Australianism that had given us Qantas or a Snowy River Scheme.

By 1956 the university had already assembled a range of 'big names' with big connections. One was Marcus Oliphant, once a father of the atomic and hydrogen bombs, now opposed to nuclear weapons. (At the ANU he tried without success to build a proton-synchrotron, a huge particle accelerator, the philosopher's stone of nuclear physics.) Another was John Eccles, the neurobiologist (later awarded the Nobel Prize for medicine). A third was Keith Hancock, the historian (who had recently completed a constitutional inquiry in Uganda. Idi Amin and Milton Obote ignored his advice.)

Among the humanist scholars the ANU may have kept in the country was John Passmore, the most famous philosopher Australia has produced since Samuel Alexander. He was the sort of Australian whose devotion to scholarship was mixed with a patriotism, almost a nationalism, characteristic of the generation that came of age in the 1920s. His Australian family line ran back to the eighteenth century and he did not see a foreign country until his early thirties when he attended a philosophy congress at Amsterdam in 1948. The debates at this congress were dominated by Bertrand Russell's polemics with Stalinist apparatchiks who wanted to enrol philosophers in the ranks of the peace-loving peoples in their struggles with the war-mongering hyenas of Wall Street. It was like a meeting of the Sydney Freethought Society.

In later years Passmore refused Chairs which would have meant compromising with the American materialism or English snobbery that as an Australian he despised. Although he has always insisted that he is not a philosopher of the first rank, everyone knows that his standard of comparison is Plato, Kant and Hegel—by which standard his colleagues are distinctly lower still.

But Passmore was *sui generis*. The ANU, it soon became clear, had become a mandarin, hierarchical establishment, obsessed with status and disdainful of the sort of open debate that might show up its limitations and pretensions. It did not take long to extrude 'trouble-makers' who believed in public controversy. Michael Lindsay (Lord Lindsay of Birker) was one who found the atmosphere at this time too oppressive: the ANU, he wrote when resigning, makes it impossible for mistakes to be corrected. It gives absolute priority to saving face. He even called it 'an evil system' that corrupts those who tolerate it.

> Occasions arise on which men must either condone actions they could not honestly defend, or else criticise decisions and cause loss of face to their colleagues. People committed to condoning indefensible behaviour are in a false position, and people in a false position behave badly . . .

Almost 30 years later, also when resigning, the sinologist and art historian Pierre Ryckmans said Lindsay's words still applied 'down to the last comma'—but so entrenched is the system that no exposure appears to make the slightest difference.

The distaste for public debate, however important the issue, showed itself soon after my arrival in the ANU's response to the Orr case. Now almost forgotten, this was in its time both sensational and portentous, as the university council in Tasmania dismissed a professor of philosophy after receiving several complaints about him from staff and students, and in particular one from the enraged father of a female student who had been Orr's lover.

Competing legends flourished around these extraordinary events.

To Orr's opponents he was a philosophic no-hoper and womaniser who should never have been appointed to the Chair. They regarded his supporters as a 'Swine's Chorus' (in the words of the poet Gwen Harwood) who used the slogan of academic freedom to destroy academic freedom in Tasmania. One of Orr's students, the artist Edwin Tanner, caught something of this view of Orr in a painting depicting him as a bat leering at a female student. (The painting is now in the Monash University collection.)

To Orr's supporters, however, he was the victim of cowardly and conservative university philistines who were revenging themselves on him for his courageous public criticisms of their administration of the university. At the least (it was said) they had denied him natural justice when hearing complaints about him. More seriously still, they were submitting him and his friends to a campaign of lies, faked evidence and brainwashing. The affair remained bitterly controversial for over ten years, with fierce polemics, bitter libels, black bans and international boycotts.

But this was for the future. I first stumbled on the issues soon after I arrived in Canberra when one wintry, sleepy Sunday morning I dragged myself along to a philosophers' conference to hear John Anderson deliver a paper entitled 'Philosophic Relations'. But with the authority that few other academics could command, he announced that he would speak to us instead about the threat to the life of inquiry signified by the summary dismissal the other day in Hobart of Sydney Sparkes Orr.

The assembled philosophers sucked their pipes, stared at the ceiling or floor or walls and barely shifted on their wooden chairs. Many wondered if the issue touched Anderson so closely because of his own deep and passionate association almost 20 years earlier with one of his students, an affair that coincided with philistine public attacks on him from parliament and pulpit.

Now he argued that the university was not *in loco parentis*; an academic was not the *servant* of an academically incompetent council but a member of a self-governing community of scholars; and the decisive consideration was the enthusiasm for learning,

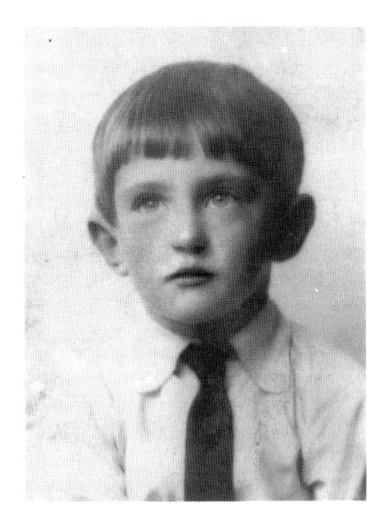

PC at 7.
A Little Boy from Melbourne.

His mother, Norma Victoria
Coleman nee Tiernan.
'Eyes often distant and lost . . .'

*PC's father, Stanley Charles Coleman,
advertising man, sometime journalist, apostle of modernity.*

*PC at 14, school cadet, as British Eighth Army
routed German Afrika Korps in May 1943. The War swung our way.*

LEFT ~ *George Munster seemed to step straight out of the Vienna of Karl Kraus and Ludwig Wittgenstein into the provincially amusing Sydney of the 1940s. He became PC's good friend.*

BELOW ~ *Verna Scott, when PC met her in 1949. They married in London in 1952.*

Donald Horne, an iconoclastic editor in the Penton tradition, started the Observer *in 1958.*

Clyde Packer was a hands-on General Manager with editorial flair.

April 19, 1958   THE OBSERVER   137

THE RISE AND FALL OF THE NOVELIST
By Peter Coleman and Robert Hughes, who apologise to Ronald Searle

Promise: *At 14 writes three-volume realistic novel based on own experience in life. Presents to teachers. Encouraged.*

Recognition: *Wins literary competition in 'Sydney Morning Herald' with novel 'The Deranged Heart,' a study of the nervous breakdown of a bushranger. Described as genius by Eric Baume.*

Success: *Acclaimed in London as voice of Common Man. Praised slightingly by Muggeridge.*

Glory: *Afternoon tea with Patrick White.*

Decline: *Appears on TV with A.A. Phillips. Advocates Chair of Australian Literature. Sales drop.*

Ruin: *Becomes President of Fellowship of Australian Writers. Visits Snowy River Scheme to collect material for next novel. Accepts Creative Writing Scholarship to U.S.A. Never heard of again.*

FACING PAGE AND ABOVE~*Robert Hughes learnt how to be an art critic on the* Observer. *He also collaborated with PC in a set of Rise and Fall cartoons (inspired by Ronald Searle).*

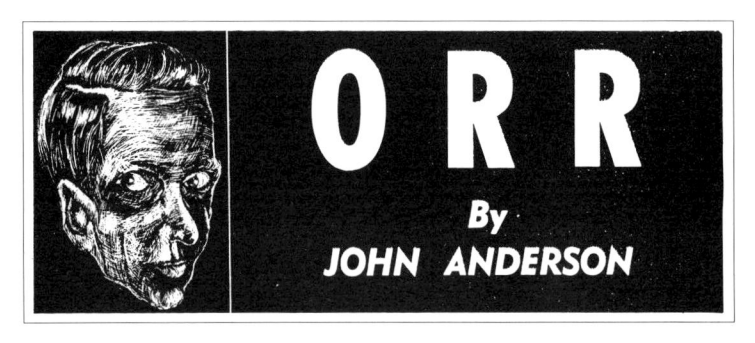

The sensational Orr case put the Observer *'on the map'. In the course of polemics, boycotts and black bans, partisans changed sides more than once.*

ABOVE~*An unknown Barry Humphries explained to readers what was wrong with Australian show business*

RIGHT~*A young Bruce Beresford used the* Observer *to publicise his plans for creating an Australian Film Industry.*

Jozef Vissel

Les Tanner, cartoonist, with PC. Tanner captured the derisive mood of the early 60s.

Frank Knopfelmacher

Many of the Observer's *political advisers came from Central Europe, including Richard Krygier* (ABOVE LEFT) *from Warsaw, Heinz Arndt* (ABOVE RIGHT) *from Breslau, and Frank Knopfelmacher* (LEFT) *from Prague. They usually disagreed on their advice.*

At the beginning of the restaurant boom in the late 1950s, dinners became a feature of Observer *life.* ABOVE (left to right): *Donald Horne, PC, Henry Mayer, Richard Krygier and Harry Glass QC.*

*Dorothy Harries, Douglas McCallum,
Verna Coleman, Owen Harries, Ann McCallum and PC.*

LEFT ~ *Patrick White, novelist.*

BELOW ~ *Barry Stern, poet and art dealer, both as seen by* Observer *illustrator Nado Milat.*

PC according to Nado Milat.

OBSERVER

April 30, 1960 — Price 1/6 — Vol. 3, No. 9

MR. INFLATION
HAWKE OF THE A.C.T.U.

Whenever PC predicted that his ANU friend Bob Hawke was bound to become Prime Minister, pundits dismissed the idea as naive. Here at the beginning of his career, Hawke gave Tanner his cover theme.

Donald Horne ridiculed Manning Clark's Meeting Soviet Man *in the* Observer, *but James McAuley* (BELOW), *still hoping that Clark would return to Christianity, was more patient with him in* Quadrant.

Not everyone was happy about the merger of the Observer *with the* Bulletin *in 1961. At the sombre party were* (ABOVE) *PC, Patricia Rolfe, Les Tanner, Donald Horne, Peter Kelly, Desmond O'Grady, Eugene Bajkowski.*

George Munster, pictured outside his office in George Street, Sydney, was the animator (with editor Tom Fitzgerald) of the Observer's *competitor,* Nation.

In 1962 the Anglican Primate of Australia, speaking from his pulpit in St Andrew's Cathedral, denounced the godless doctrines taught, mainly by John Anderson, in the philosophy school at Sydney University. The public debate was a debacle – and a turning point for PC.

ABOVE~*John Anderson, by Nado Milat.*

LEFT~*The Archbishop as seen by Tanner.*

OBSERVER

Registered at the G.P.O., Sydney, for transmission by post as a newspaper.

March 18, 1961   Price 1/6   Vol. 4, No. 6

or grave thy victory?

THE DEATH OF THE OBSERVER

BURIAL NOTICE PAGE 3

Robert Hughes' illustration for the last issue of the Observer *originally was a small decorative dinkus drawn a couple of years earlier for 10s 6d. Vastly 'blown up' for the cover, it caught the spirit of the occasion.*

the love of philosophy that characterised Sydney Sparkes Orr. Anderson's austere demagoguery certainly impressed me (and others in the audience including the renowned English philosopher Gilbert Ryle who later referred to the University of Tasmania as 'that loony bin'). We readily passed resolutions supporting Orr morally and financially.

But at the Australian National University the issue was almost immediately dropped. Many indeed supported the university council in Tasmania. Orr was, they said, clearly a 'trouble-maker'. The last thing anyone wanted was scrutiny of university decisions. The general unwillingness, even refusal, to discuss the issues made me feel I could have no future in such a place. As it turned out, I later changed my views on the Orr case almost entirely, but this was the result of long and public discussion and owed nothing to the 'scholars and humanists' of the ANU.

The ANU's response to the Cold War at this time was just as dispiriting if more enterprising. We had arrived in Canberra on the very day in 1956 when the world's newspapers carried reports of Mr Khrushchev's devastating 'secret speech' in Moscow denouncing, however selectively, Stalin's crimes—the murders, tortures, false confessions, show trials, and mass arrests.

Soon millions of prisoners were being released from prison camps and millions more posthumously rehabilitated. The old head of the Soviet Writers' Union, Alexander Fadeyev, shot himself in May and the literary sensation in Russia was a new novel, Vladimir Dudintsev's *Not by Bread Alone*, portraying the contest of an honest man with the corrupt Communist Party. The thaw spread across the whole Soviet bloc. It was an *annus mirabilis*.

The ANU scholars, always contemptuous of anti-communist polemics, welcomed these developments as marking the end of the Cold War. Some also sensibly wanted to do what they could to encourage further liberalisation in the communist countries. One of the first moves was to send a delegation of academics, writers and painters to China. This was the time of the Peking thaw—when the Hundred Flowers were to bloom.

This sort of 'cultural exchange' was always a matter for tact and judgment in those years. If you wanted to reach fellow spirits in communist countries, you had to go through the painful business of being courteous to all sorts of petty frauds and sinister hacks—which often involved a sense of betraying your principles. But if, out of solidarity with writers struggling against dictatorship, you refused to deal with the apparatchiks at all, you gave up an opportunity of reaching your friends.

I cannot claim that I always made the right judgment in my coping with this problem. In the late 1960s I was booked to visit Moscow on a 'cultural mission'—to look at their film school—but I finally decided not to go. In 1969 the memory of Soviet suppression of the Prague Spring was still too much for my stomach. In one of his memoirs, Gough Whitlam, the hero of the Baltic states and Central Europe, laughed at my petty scruples, and I have sometimes regretted my decision. But I have always admired Solzhenitsyn's judgment on cultural exchanges when he refused to meet Jean-Paul Sartre in Moscow because he knew that Sartre would try to use the meeting as evidence of the cultural freedom in the USSR.

It would be foolish to criticise those who went to China in 1956. One simply does not know what private contacts they made. But to return from a routine guided tour, as Partridge did—the same teacher (and friend) who had so effectively dismissed Soviet propaganda in the 1940s—and proclaim a great renaissance in Mao's China, a land of new freedom, stability and excitement, was for me a disheartening spectacle. No-one doubted the integrity of the tourists, only their judgment. They were vintage victims of the Eye Witness Fallacy. Soon after their visit, Mao launched the Great Leap Forward, a new age of ferocious persecution, regimentation and ruin.

Almost as depressing was Manning Clark's visit to Russia. He seemed to me, after I had settled down in Canberra, to be one of the few voices to speak out against the spiritual vanity and vacuity of the secular faiths of both the left and the right. I heard his public lecture, called 'A Democrat on the Ganges', about his recent tour in Asia. The march of modernity in the East, he said, threatened to make all Asia look like the Canberra suburbs, Turner or Braddon, but Islam, Buddhism and Hinduism still had more resources to resist modernity than the feeble faiths of the West, especially Protestantism.

He went to Russia soon after the suppression of the Hungarian revolution and the renewed attacks on Boris Pasternak. On his return he repeated mean-spirited jibes at people like Silone who had supported Hungarian writers. He even managed to describe some miserable hounders of Pasternak as new Elizabethans. He appeared to abandon all restraint when he met Alexei Surkov, the secretary of the Writers' Union, a position reserved for the most reliable apparatchiks always willing to 'explain' the suicide, internment or execution of a Russian writer. Surkov had already sacked the courageous editor Alexander Tvardovsky, denounced the anti-Stalinist novelist Vladimir Dudintsev, and led the pack against Boris Pasternak. Clark found him to be, like Tolstoy, a man of 'earthy images and folk wisdom' . . . 'a great man, a very great man'. I was baffled and unable to reconcile this Manning Clark with the man I thought I knew.

Who was there to speak for the liberal West in this wasteland? There were one or two. Eugene Kamenka always remained sceptical about the Soviet Union until its collapse. I also went with Bob Hawke to some debates on the Russian developments in the Parliament, where the politicians seemed better informed than most of the academics at the ANU. Most dramatic of all was an address which B. A. Santamaria gave at Canberra University College in May 1956. His intensity—laced with dry humour—stunned the packed hall.

But the ANU mandarins were unmoved. Inevitably they ignored the visit to Canberra of the legendary American novelist James T. Farrell—author of the *Studs Lonigan* trilogy and a famous polemic *The League of Frightened Philistines*, which brought a sort of New York or Chicago Trotskyism to the critique of cultural Stalinism.

I had expected a great deal from his visit and had enjoyed his new book of short stories, *French Girls Are Vicious*, especially 'They Ain't the Men They Used to Be', which is about an old baseball fan who, now that the great contests are over, has nothing more to live for—but at another level it is also an autobiographical comment on anyone who puts his faith in creeds like Stalinism or Trotskyism: 'It was the loneliest thing I ever saw, those empty stands in the darkness. Well, that's it. There's nothing more for me to say.' I was reminded of this story by the desolation of both communists and anti-communists after the end of the Cold War, as they asked themselves: what now?

Farrell was in a gloomy mood when he reached Australia. He was one of the series of speakers brought here by Richard Krygier and the Australian Committee for Cultural Freedom. (Stephen Spender and Malcolm Muggeridge had done the tour earlier. Generally the English left behind a warmer impression than did the Americans, who always seemed to be asking themselves what the hell they were doing in this barren and ridiculous outpost.)

I met Farrell at a reception arranged by Arthur Trendall, the Master of University House. A heavy-set, broad-chested Irish-American, he was a drunk and a womaniser (although he had recently remarried his divorced first wife). Always with him was a short plump man who, I could not help noticing, would promptly quaff the drinks that the waiter kept pouring for Farrell. It turned out to be Richard Krygier, who hoped by this stratagem to stop Farrell becoming drunk, aggressive and a militantly patriotic Americaniser. It did not always succeed. Very few turned up for the reception. The Canberra academics dismissed him as a Cold Warrior and did not care about his literary achievement.

He talked to Bob Hawke about the Labor Party and told him that he had recently broadcast to Russian trade unionists on the Voice of America urging them to get stuck into the Communist

Party. Hawke smiled faintly at Farrell but remained silent.

He also questioned Trendall, the Master, about the relentless press harassment of the composer Eugene Goossens who had just now been charged with importing a collection of pornographic photographs and a set of masks for black masses. Who, he asked, was Rosaleen Norton? Why was no one speaking up for Goossens the artist? Was there a conspiracy of silence? (There was. Barry Humphries told me he had written a sketch for the Phillip Street Theatre lampooning the Sydney press for its harassment of Goossens. But the theatre thought it best to say nothing. It strengthened Humphries in his determination to leave Australia.)

Farrell gave me his acerbic run-down on American writers. Hemingway, he said, was past it. Steinbeck oversimplified everything. He didn't like Raymond Chandler. When I asked him what Nelson Algren thought about Simone de Beauvoir's account of their affair in *The Mandarins*, he quoted Algren's jibe that even in a whorehouse a woman usually closes the door.

That night he spoke on American literary realism to a tiny audience. He came most to life when he talked about a novel that I had not heard of: Harold Frederic's *The Damnation of Theron Ware*, about a small-town Protestant minister who destroys himself in his doomed attempts to cope with modernity as represented by a liberal Catholic, a Darwinian scientist and a feminist woman. Farrell was really talking about himself, an Irish boy from the south side of Chicago, and his inability to cope with the intellectual currents of his time.

His tour was a flop. Old enemies, *the frightened philistines* of the left, boycotted him and the conservatives had little interest in him in the first place. But part of the problem was Farrell's moodiness—aggressive, uncertain, alcoholic. He was a lost soul. In Melbourne he fell into public polemics with Stalinists who were hardly worth his trouble. In Sydney he spoke from the platform in Sydney Town Hall in support of a Chair of Australian literature but made dim remarks about Australian writers as frontier humorists—in the year of new novels by Patrick White,

Randolph Stow, Martin Boyd and Hugh Atkinson, none of whom he had read or was going to read.

He left Australia depressed by his own performance and by the anti-Americanism that was seemed a datum among the *bien pensants*. After similar experiences in Delhi, Karachi and Istanbul, his rage exploded in a drunken but heartfelt letter he sent to the *Chicago Tribune*, an isolationist and right-wing newspaper in his home town that had always opposed everything he had stood for. 'We honest Americans,' he wrote, 'have had enough of the blood of our boys spilled on foreign soil. From here on in, we should have an honest partnership in freedom or else go it alone . . . retire to our own shores and if necessary fight to the death with communism.'

Later he drew an entirely different moral from his tour—that American anti-communism was doomed in Asia. The truth is he didn't know what he believed any more and, like his baseball fan in the short story, he had nothing left to say. Since I have often felt in the same mood myself, his confusion—perhaps it should be called a breakdown—did not reduce my respect for him and his books.

At about the same time I put on an amateur production of John Osborne's love story *Look Back in Anger*. It is a pretentious play, yet its frequent revival (with Richard Burton, Malcolm McDowell and lately Kenneth Branagh as Jimmy Porter) shows that it captures something of the groping heart-ache of the young, caught between decaying old values and horrible new ones (in this case, between a grand old socialism and an awful new consumerism). James Dean's doomed boy (in *Rebel without a Cause*), William Holden's drifter (*Picnic*) and Tony Curtis's press agent (*Sweet Smell of Success*) also caught the various moods—idealism, despair, self-disgust—of the 1950s young, including my own.

My first daughter was born in Canberra—the joyful moment in an otherwise discouraging year—and I was now determined to leave the ANU. But how? This was the moment of a very depressing visit to Canberra by V. Gordon Childe, the great archaeologist who was probably most widely honoured for his youthful critique of socialist opportunism, *How Labor Governs*—a classic text of radical idealism that still leaves its own vanities unexamined. There was even less hope in Australia now, he said gloomily, than when he had first left it. P. R. Stephensen told me that he had taken Childe, one of his old teachers from Maryborough Grammar, to lunch. Childe had always encouraged him, he said, in his *contra mundum* outlook. I would like to have been a fly on the wall. It would have been a sad comedy to have heard these two casualties of the twentieth century—the fascist and the communist—discuss what Childe called their 'indiscretions'.

Then Childe was found dead at the foot of a cliff near Katoomba. He had climbed over a safety fence, left his hat, coat, glasses, pipe and compass at the edge of the cliff and ended his life.

Suddenly Bob Hawke—one of those whose own indiscretions, evasions, strange intensities, blindnesses and charm—had helped make my Canberra days tolerable, decided to leave the Australian National University and become a 'research officer' at the trade unions' headquarters in Melbourne. His real career had begun.

I spent an evening in Melbourne with him before he made his final decision. We went to a pub in Lygon Street that displayed faded pictures of sundry political hacks or heroes on its walls and then to a party across the road at the offices of a long since abolished union where drunk officials sang snatches about the bush, the wild west and the deep south. When Hawke drove us home, he shot along St Kilda Road hunched over the wheel peering moodily through rimless glasses. At the Junction he swung into orbit and spun around the circus a dozen times looking for the right exit, the right way home. Each time as we sped past I would call out: 'There it is! There!'—each time too late. Then, by luck or intuition, he suddenly shot off at a tangent up the right turn-off. He dropped me home and I last saw him rocketing towards Sandringham.

There was something epiphanous about it. Pugnacious, ambitious, full of confidence, in a hell of a hurry, not certain where to turn but not listening to advice. He had several choices—the

Labor Party, the university, the trade unions. He made the right choice. The next time I visited him in Melbourne, he sooled an Alsatian dog on me.

But what of me? What was my future? How much longer could I go on drifting in this Sargasso Sea? Suddenly Donald Horne threw me a life-belt—a new fortnightly magazine of radical–conservative ideas, price 1s 6d. A fiddle for eighteenpence!

PART THREE

A Fiddle for Eighteenpence

When I was young and had no sense,
I bought a fiddle for eighteenpence.
But the only tune that I could play
Was Over the Hills and Far Away
                Irish Children's Song

CHAPTER 7

Starting a New Magazine

The building was a decaying pile, almost ready for the wreckers. But it was the right address—Adams Chambers, Elizabeth Street, facing Hyde Park. I took a creaking goods lift to the fourth floor. Donald Horne—dandiacal, in an English suit—was sitting behind a triangular desk ('Red Ted's,' he said. 'Theodore's.') littered with legal papers. He was in the mode of quiet fury.

Someone in Brisbane had tipped off his company—Australian Consolidated Press—that the Queensland censors intended to ban *Weekend*, the *louche*, lively and popular weekly he edited. The company had obtained a restraining injunction and briefed the awesome Garfield Barwick, QC, to fight the proposed ban. 'I'm going to see Archbishop Mannix,' Horne hissed with puritanical anger. 'Read this.' He handed me a legal opinion on the powers of the Queensland Literature Board of Review. As I glanced through it, journalists came and went with *Weekend* page proofs. ('No!' was Horne's usual reaction.) The phone rang. ('Tell him to get fucked!') Someone poked his head in the door. ('You're sacked.') A copy boy brought us coffee. ('Piss off!') Everyone enjoyed the show.

But it was hard to take a righteous interest in *Weekend*'s battle for freedom of speech. In those days I yielded to few in calling for the total abolition of censorship of all kinds. (One of my little triumphs in Canberra had been to help make a public issue of the Commonwealth ban on J. D. Salinger's *Catcher in the Rye*, which the U.S. ambassador had just donated to the library at University House.) I knew the routine argument that once you ban one thing, you will end up banning everything. I had used it myself. But I never really believed it. In any case *Weekend* still seemed an unlikely ally of James Joyce or Vladimir Nabokov.

But Horne was obsessed. Suddenly he gazed at me. His lips moved. I could not hear anything. I leaned forward. I still heard nothing. His lips were still moving. I cupped my ear and wondered: Am I having a stroke? Horne frowned impatiently and raised his voice irritably. Until this Queensland affair was all over, he whispered, he would have no time for the *Observer*. I should see Clyde Packer, George Baker, Francis James and the others. They would fill me in.

Clyde Packer was 22, fresh-faced and heavy. He did not whisper. He preferred to bellow. Hammering his desk with a large fist, he shouted: 'The *Observer* should back the colonels in Sumatra!' (The colonels were mounting an insurrection against Sukarno's dictatorship in Jakarta. The CIA was sponsoring it, but despite that—or because of it—the rebellion was doomed from the start.) 'Think what it would mean to the magazine if we put them in power!' I nodded without complete conviction. 'I'm sick to death of Australia's rabbit diplomacy!' he went on. 'Canberra thinks that if Australia is a good, quiet rabbit and sits still, no one will shoot at us! Do you *believe* that?'

Before I could find an answer, he turned again to Dr Sukarno. 'I think the *Observer* should invite the big boong here! We could bung on a banquet for him. And a State dinner in King's Hall. Menzies could give him a gong from the Queen! It would put the *Observer* on the map. And the Boong would be on side for life. Or for a while anyhow. What do you reckon?'

Fortunately his secretary interrupted to say that Malcolm Muggeridge wanted him to come to lunch at the Yacht Club. I withdrew to allow Mr Muggeridge a voice in shaping the *Observer*'s— or Australia's—foreign policy.

Across the corridor George Baker, an obese, tense homosexual who was an assistant editor of the *Observer*, sat with a sour crone, his secretary. They both stared at me with open contempt. Baker was convinced that Horne had brought me in as part of a plot to frustrate Baker's own plot to eliminate Horne.

'What school did you go to?' he asked with disdain. 'What is your Church?' Before I could answer, he told me he was an Anglican. High Church. 'The best lack all conviction,' he sighed, 'and the worst are full of passionate intensity.' The crone grinned. He tossed at me a draft design for the cover of the *Observer*. 'What do you think?' It was a mess of busy fanciness, as if a thousand dainty flies had dragged themselves across the page. The crone grinned again as I examined the page in a deep study.

Baker was above all an anglophile and the great period of his life had been his war years in England when he had been, he conveyed, one of the few, indeed the few within the few, in that he had responded to England's call across the seas even as far as the outback of New South Wales. Later, when I came to feel some sympathy for his obviously tortured temperament, he lent me his copy of Don Charlwood's *No Moon Tonight* about the brave Australians in the Battle of Britain and showed me drafts of some of his London poems, including a ballad about his first sexual encounter with a woman—a prostitute in High Holborn during the Blitz: her aspen ardour, he wrote, gave him some brief courage. It had a deft pathos and I urged Jim McAuley to put it in *Quadrant*. In the end he did.

'You'd better meet Francis James,' Baker said. 'Our printer. The Anglican Press. Bring that cover design.' We took a taxi to Chippendale while Baker recited *The Four Quartets*. At the printery, Francis James took one look at me, jumped to his feet and battered the wall with his head, wailing: 'Another damned intellectual!' Then, turning around, he asked: 'What school did you go to, my boy?' Donning a ten-gallon cowboy hat, he showed me over the new presses that would print the *Observer*.

'It takes flair to handle the working class,' he shouted over the din. 'I know! I used to be one of them.'

He handed me a page proof of an *Anglican* editorial supporting *Weekend* in its battle with the Queensland censors: 'Insupportable arrogance . . . Papal inquisition . . . Roman jurisprudence . . . British justice.' Before I left, he stood in a corner with Baker tensely whispering about 'Horne . . . Noumea . . . Clyde . . . McNicoll . . .'

Soon a face-saving formula was found to settle the *Weekend* dispute. Australian Consolidated Press agreed to make changes to *Weekend* and the Queensland Board of Review congratulated itself on bringing about some reform. But you still needed a keen eye to pick the changes in *Weekend*.

Horne took a cruise to Noumea and for a couple of weeks I sat at my desk in Elizabeth Street doing nothing while Baker and his crone glared at me in silent hostility. When Horne was due back, Clyde Packer suggested we all go down to the wharf to welcome him home. I was surprised by this unexpected warmth, but it blossomed into a paroxysm of joy and delight as Packer, Baker and Horne embraced each other on the wharf.

In these high spirits we all returned to the office, where Packer sacked Horne and announced that Baker would replace him as editor of the *Observer*. Horne thereupon resigned as editor of *Weekend*. He only agreed to return when he was reappointed to the *Observer* and Baker was sacked as its editor. The coup and counter-coup were at least quicker than the colonels' coup in Sumatra.

In this bracing atmosphere, we at last got on with the business of preparing the first issue of the new magazine. It was a disaster. It began with a preposterous editorial drafted by Baker and rewritten in a last minute rush by Horne, Packer and anyone with a spare moment. It was about the Russian threat to Australian Antarctica! 'In no less than four places the Red Flag now flies over the ice of our southern Territory. We are going to have the devil's own job getting the Russians out.' At least someone had the good sense to give the editorial the ironic title: 'We Warn the Tsar'. (It also ceded the Falklands to Argentina, but no-one worried about that!)

Inside the magazine the major articles included a silly blast from George Baker at the racketeering in the Australian National University (which, being unsigned, was going to be attributed to me), and a better piece by George Munster on the battles of the new soap powders (*Tide, Surf, Daz, Dreft, Omo*) which rehearsed his later, more famous essays on the wars and plots of big business.

Charles Higham gave a disenchanted view of London's Angry Young Men: 'On their faces you can see the marks of the intellectual jungle they inhabit. Only Mr [Kenneth] Tynan, looking boozy, seems at all gay. Socialism has yielded him rich rewards.'

Horne did an idiosyncratic and perceptive review of Patrick White's *Voss*: 'At its best it is a nightmare exposition of what men are like. At its worst it is a nightmare example of how a novel or a note to the milkman should not be written.' Voss, who claimed he wanted to explore an empty continent, really wanted to be God 'along with a few other lunatic odds and ends'. But in Horne's view all great men are mad and life is a mad expedition. Perhaps he was thinking of the *Observer*.

My own contributions included a suitably Dada report, suggested by Baker who rewrote it, on the Australian role in the Sudan wars! 'You have a great future with the RSL,' Packer told me. '*Reveille* needs you!'

To complete the farce the *Anglican* printers could not work the new machinery and the first issue rolled off the press with pages upside down and in the wrong order. At 4 a.m. they informed Francis James, who had been trying to get some sleep on a couch. He donned his ten-gallon hat and, otherwise stark naked, joined the rest of us squatting on the printery floor to work out what had gone wrong.

Perce Partridge, who like most of the Canberra academics had warned me against having anything to do with the Packer press, took the trouble to drop me a line about the first issue. He could find only 'intellectual seediness or spivishness . . . Much of it is juvenile . . . there isn't an article that suggests that the writer knows what he is talking about . . . the depressing stamp of a not very bright undergraduate . . . hardly reaches the level of *Honi Soit* . . .' and so on.

I passed the letter around and, although we all scoffed at Partridge's 'stuffiness', we knew that he was at least half right. Yet there was vitality, however badly directed, and some intelligence in the *Observer* that should have been apparent to a reader like

Partridge. But little could be done in the atmosphere of gang warfare. In the end, Baker's supporters abandoned him, and one morning he packed up and left. He drifted for a couple of years around the fringes of journalism, television and politics and then, a dying man, killed himself with an overdose of heroin.

Back in Adams Chambers, we could try once again to make some dint in the history of our time. I'd also had my fill of the malevolence that often attends the management of magazines.

Donald Horne now emerged as an editor of infectious gaiety. He wore several masks. One was the quiet disgust of a man overburdened by the venal mediocrities on his staff. (This was often assumed before dropping someone's copy into a waste basket as if disposing of a soiled diaper.) Another was frenzied rage, his patience with the office cheats, drunks and loafers finally exhausted. (Then he would sack one or two. Birthdays or Christmas Eve were good times. He would take the precaution of having the office bruiser stand beside him.) Still another was the mimic who delighted in charades spoofing the Pecksniffs, parasites and *pomposi* of church and state, big business and universities. (Militant journalists, Labor politicians, Marxist intellectuals and academic hacks were favourite butts.)

He read widely and savagely—not like the common reader, more like an artist seizing on bits and pieces that helped him at the moment. (He would find them anywhere—a play by Anouilh, a novel by Anthony Powell, a biography of Horatio Bottomley . . .) He responded eagerly to new talent, unlike those editors whose main preoccupation is to suppress talent or silence rivals. A pamphleteer in the English tradition, his lively anarchism was restrained only by a weaknesss for heroes—at this period Frank Packer. (It was Frank Packer's later sacking him that led, I am sure, to his shift to the left.)

Although called the *Observer*, the magazine could have been called *Polemic*, since each issue set out to portray Australia as a dun country run by second-raters and their toadies.

Michael Baume, now in the Senate but then frustrated at the

Australian Financial Review, was the first to join us—as an associate editor. (The title meant little. You could call yourself anything. Horne had an appealing contempt for such *frou-frou*. He had no doubt in the world, he told us, that Frank Packer would never accept a knighthood!) Baume was a finance journalist who wrote on everything from opera to soccer—under his various pseudonyms. He also won our first writ for defamation (over his exposure of a New Guinea coffee company) and danced with pride when some smirk served the writ.

He was one of the early exponents of 'investigative journalism'. 'It's all crap,' he would say. 'It's so easy. All you need are leaks and a telephone. There's plenty of both.' In a more po-faced mood, he might add: 'Wherever there are factions, there are dissatisfactions. The price of liberty is eternal treachery.' He had leaks in everything from the Australian Broadcasting Commission to the Knights of the Southern Cross. He even had them in the ultra-secretive Australian Journalists' Association. His report from inside the masonic lodges was the first and still the best of its kind in Australia. Baume's versatility—along with some casual help, including briefly the humorist 'Buzz' Kennedy—rounded out our forward platoon. But what put us on the map was Sydney Sparkes Orr and the *Observer*'s espousal of the cause that had been so easily brushed aside at the ANU.

The Orr case had everything . . . mediocre academics and establishment lawyers covering up the shabby mistreatment of a freethinking philosopher and possibly a miscarriage of justice. Here were the great Australian frauds, the comfortable, highly placed, mean and pompous second-raters concealing a great scandal. This was the theme that the *Observer* made its own over the next three years—the Independent versus the Establishment. But none of the later exemplars had the salience of the Orr case, which also had the advantage of dividing the country—with John Anderson and the philosophers on one side, and John Kerr, QC, and the Tasmanian Supreme Court on the other.

Robert Hughes did a striking portrait of Orr as the cover for our first major issue on the case (his debut as a cover designer) and we were unrelenting in our campaign—reporting the libels, exposing the suppression of evidence, ridiculing the fear of debate. We never went as far as some of Orr's partisans like Harry Eddy, who had made a study of communist brainwashing techniques in Korean prisoner-of-war camps and saw similar techniques at work in Hobart. But we did not let up.

Until, that is, we began to have doubts . . . when it became clear that the issues were developing into more than a contest between the Orr forces of Light and the anti-Orr forces of Darkness. A new struggle for power emerged between those in the Orr camp who, regardless of the truth, were using the case to assert the authority of teachers against administrators, and those in the anti-Orr camp who saw worker-control and academic boycotts as marking the end of traditional universities. This was not the issue that had drawn us to the case.

My own dealings with Orr and some of his supporters also gave me pause. Once I had to taxi him around Sydney in my car and it was disconcerting to hear him refer to himself in the third person. 'Orr', he would say 'maintains . . .' and 'In Orr's opinion . . .' More importantly, he also made it clear that he was not going to be satisfied with a financial settlement and restoration to his Chair. He wanted nothing less than a top-to-bottom purge of Tasmanian society, a sort of social and political revolution. He had found a new career—and one that no longer engaged my sympathy.

Around this time John Kerr, QC, and Hal Wootten had published a weighty critique of Orr's legal arguments. But when I began to discuss it with one of Orr's champions, Professor Alan Stout, he cried: 'I can't read it! I just can't bring myself to look at it!'

Gradually the weight of argument forced us to retreat. I summed up my growing scepticism in a piece which said that the case now depended on Harry Eddy's forthcoming book, *Orr*. It would either reopen it in a root-and-branch way or show that there was nothing left to reopen. When I read and I reviewed the book, I found it unconvincing.

We still insisted that Orr had been denied natural justice. (No due notice when he was sacked. No opportunity to mount a case or scrutinise the evidence against him.) We also continued to oppose the boycott of the university. But the affair finally ended when Orr, on his death bed, accepted a financial settlement. The boycott was lifted and the academic study of philosophy resumed in Tasmania.

The *Observer* survived these shifting debates and prospered in them. But one of the great casualties was Orr's champion, Harry Eddy. The campaign over so many years exhausted him and contributed to his death in 1973.

I was surprised at first to see that his funeral service was at Moore Theological College—although this was where he had lived as a student before becoming a freethinker under the influence of John Anderson. I was even more surprised to see Archbishop Sir Marcus Loane enter the pulpit to deliver a final tribute. He told how, on his death bed, Eddy had asked to see him, how they had prayed together and how Eddy had murmured: 'Christ will carry me through'. This moved me more than I would then publicly admit.

CHAPTER 8
New Critics

Newspapers at this time never devoted full pages, let alone whole departments, exclusively to the arts. Sport and finance had their own sections, but shows and performances were treated as news, and the notices were slotted in with the politics, crimes and bushfires. This may be the better way of treating them, but we didn't think so in 1958 when the *Observer* began devoting a major section of each issue to the arts. We had no programme or doctrine beyond looking for whatever was hot and rebellious. Our first major contributor was the art critic Robert Hughes.

Bob Hughes was a tall, blond, bluff youth who, adopting the role of impatient and overbearing artist, knocked on the office door to ask . . . if we could perhaps use an illustrator . . . freelance . . . cheap . . . We took him on. He began with a few dinkuses and satiric motifs. They showed promise. Then he and I collaborated on some cartoon stories modelled on Ronald Searle's Rise and Fall series. These showed even greater promise. Next he moved into cover design—and his cover on the Orr case sold the issue.

Above all he wanted to move into art criticism, although we already had a critic in Bernard Hesling, a talented writer–artist–cartoonist. But Hesling never liked his perch on the *Observer* and regarded its rate of payment as an insult calculated to reduce him to tears or even bring on a seizure. Bob Hughes did not care about all that. He would have done the job for nothing. He soon got the job.

His début was at the exhibition in Sydney of the Hiroshima Panels, eight large, gross cartoons coarsely memorialising the victims of the first atomic bomb. They exploited and even degraded an unspeakable horror. But they were the talk, if not the toast of the town, as they were wherever they were exhibited around the world. Always sensitive to current opinion, Hughes shamelessly described the panels as better than Picasso's 'Guernica'. He never looked back, but he never made such a foolish misjudgment again.

His reviews of Australian artists were far more detached and critical. He described Albert Tucker's 'Australian Gothic' as 'cynical and brilliantly ruthless' and Bob Dickerson's morbid faces as 'stuck in a rut that may deepen into a grave'. (He boasted that an enraged Dickerson had flattened him in a pub and that Tucker was looking for him with a gun.) Jack Lynn's paint, he said, cannot cover 'the banality of his vision' and Arthur Boyd or Leonard French will give you no sense of discovery once you have enjoyed Léger or Chagall. But if you want a little Gleghorn for the bathroom or an Elaine Haxton watercolour to match your sofa, go quickly to the new exhibition at Macquarie Galleries.

'Mr Gleghorn's work,' he wrote, 'can usually be counted on to have the orchidaceous allure of a Venus fly-trap . . . the stimulus is to immediate pleasure rather than to thought'. Jon Molvig 'serves up some singularly unappetising mud pies'. John Olsen's pictographs and thick slabs of paint are 'going to kill abstract art . . . you could remove the title from any one of the pictures, give it another, and be able to read entirely different meanings into it'.

Hughes was soon celebrated around Sydney as a critic, artist, illustrator, poet. His enemies were quick to dismiss him as a poor artist, an imitative illustrator and a plagiarising poet. They were all, Hughes said, absolutely right. But he had a courage and an independence that have almost entirely disappeared as critics have increasingly become part of what Horne used to call the Great Australian Culture Fraud, now subsidised. The *Observer* created Robert Hughes. Since then he has become the most widely read art critic in the world and his cool, comic and committed judgments in *Time* magazine have directed the taste of millions.

Finding our film critic was a tougher ordeal. Australian film culture was still feeble and Australian film-making dormant. There was no film magazine, no film school, no private investment, no government assistance. The leading directors and actors, cameramen and designers continued to leave the country. Yet the Australian 'film generation' was beginning to emerge and form a market. We wanted to cater for them. Again we were lucky. Another young man—tall, tousled, square-shouldered, corduroyed, about 19—poked his head in the door. Were we interested in the problems of Australian film-makers? His name was Bruce Beresford.

He had just been to ask Frank Packer for a hand-out to help him make a feature film about Everyman and the Devil. Packer agreed and David McNicoll sent Beresford to talk to me about writing for the *Observer*. He soon let us know his views: The trouble with Australian films has always been their mindlessness. We made 160 feature films in the silent era and only *The Sentimental Bloke* was still worth seeing. Since then, we had made about 90 talkies, but they were without exception well below the standards of films made abroad. While we were making Dad and Dave comedies, the Americans were making masterpieces like *Grand Hotel*. We go on blaming the exhibitors or distributors or our lack of technical resources. But the only essential ingredient of good films is good ideas. In 60 years of making films, no Australian producer, apart from the Salvation Army which made *Soldiers of the Cross* in 1900, had taken on a worthwhile theme. Once you have ideas, all you need is a second-hand Bolex.

Beresford agreed to write up all this up for the *Observer*, and the resulting manifesto—we called it 'Why Australian Films Are So Bad'—remains the best statement of the complaints and hopes of the emerging young directors who some ten years later would become an Australian New Wave—a movement which in the 1970s won the world's respect.

Beresford invited me to join a group of actors, poets and dancers for a private screening, at a friend's home in Castlecrag, of *The Hunter*, a short film he had just shot, written and directed. The audience included the actor John Bell, the poet Donovan

Clarke and the balletomane Anton Sedlar. Beresford had made *The Hunter* as a silent film—16 mm, black and white, seven minutes—and dubbed in bird sounds and folk music later. It begins with an idyllic bush scene into which strides a young man with a rifle who kills everything in sight. Flies buzz around his digger hat and a dog chews a dead kangaroo's leg. It ends with dead branches pleading and mad birds screeching. There were obvious influences of John Ford and Akira Kurosawa. But it was also the apprentice work of a master artist.

Beresford would not at that stage write about the longer film he was then directing and producing at Sydney University—*The Devil to Pay*, about a desperate young man who sells his soul for a life of wealth, women and fame, but no love. It won some sort of award and Frank Packer showed it late one night on his television stations in Sydney and Melbourne. Many of the 30 student actors and technicians became well known figures in the industry—John Bell, actor; Peter Butler, composer; John Coburn, artist; Peter Fenton, sound mixer; Richard Brennan, producer; Michael Newman, writer; and Richard Keyes, cameraman.

But Beresford soon disowned *The Devil to Pay*. 'It's terrible! Far worse than the films people of my age were making in other countries at that time.' When I told him years later that one major library had, in a clean-out of old material, destroyed a damaged print of *The Devil to Pay*, he was delighted. 'I wish all the libraries would destroy their prints!'

He wrote for us from time to time, but although he saw every film ever made in the world, and made copious notes about them all, they were director's notes and he never became a reviewer. He only began to write seriously on films after he joined the British Film Institute in the late 1960s and published his (still uncollected) studies of directors from George Stevens to Kenneth Anger and of genres from Errol Flynn swashbucklers to John Ford westerns . . .

His review for the *Observer* of Tim Burstall's first film *The Prize* (1959) catches the feel of Australian film-making 35 years ago. A

45 minute children's tale about getting back a stolen goat, *The Prize* stars the director's son Tom and 'a charming little scene-stealer' named Lisa Jacka. Its moral is the importance of self-help.

> The makers had nothing to assist their enthusiasm but primitive equipment and lack of money. As all the sound had to be dubbed, dialogue was cut to a minimum (100 words) and as no narration was used, characterisations suffer.
> Mr Burstall lacked experience to use the camera creatively to capture moods and expressions. Gerard Vandenberg's background as a still photographer is obvious. His close-ups and compositions are excellent but nothing is conveyed of the vastness and grandeur of the countryside. Dorian Le Gallienne's [stunning] music score is used too insistently. Where natural bush sounds could have conveyed a mood, the score swings, soars and crashes . . .
> Not an all-round success, the film is a step towards a school of film technique which is Australian in flavour . . .

Charles Higham, later a prolific Hollywood biographer, seemed for a moment to be the answer to our problem. A neo-romantic poet and refugee from the mean London of the early 1950s, he would recall with a shudder its sulphur fogs, its low, dark skies . . . and its dank critics in raincoats: 'It was like living in a cave'. Arriving in Australia was like walking into the Uffizi Gallery—the colour and light, the rich produce, the harsh, welcoming voices. His years in Sydney were a formative period in his life and he would always speak of his debt to John Olsen and Robert Hughes (who introduced him to art: he had never met a painter in England), to Jim McAuley (who taught him discipline and shared his passion for French symbolists), to Roland Robinson (who ignited his sense of the supernatural: 'I felt what it would be like to die') and Patrick White (who encouraged him as a poet).

George Baker recruited him as a book reviewer for the *Observer* but he was really obsessed with films, especially films as images. He once brought tears to the eyes of the great Hollywood cameraman James Wong Howe with his total recall of images Howe had created thirty years before.

But, like Beresford, Higham was too idiosyncratic to be the critic we needed. He had no more interest in new waves than in old silent films. He thought foreign films far inferior to American. He didn't care for 'that Swede' (Bergman) or the Italian (Fellini) or the Frenchman (Truffaut). He was sceptical about the prospects for Australian film: *What* directors or cameramen? As for local actors, a visit to a Sydney theatre would always send him home in *despair*. He gave us a few pieces on the decline and fall of the great Hollywood studios—the theme he developed into his book *Hollywood at Sunset*—and moved on. We were still looking . . .

Martin Long—composer, novelist, and journalist—finally solved our problem. He understood the small Australian film world from the inside—and had scored some films, including one for his wife Joan Long. (He had also composed the music for one of Warwick Fairfax's plays.) Unlike Beresford, he was not too busy making his own films. Unlike Higham, he was excited by the new directors in Poland, England and France. For most of our readers—and certainly for me—he was the main guide to all the new waves.

We faced the same problem yet again with theatre and drama. Remember we were feeling our way, without doctrine or dogma. We wanted simply to join forces with whatever lively elements we could find in contemporary theatre. The problem was there were not many to find. It was a shoddy period. Hal Porter said at this time that there was better theatre at the races or on the beach than on the Australian stage. The standard fare was still a microwaved West End production. The new 'intimate revue' had already lost its bite and was plagiarising its London models or sucking up to 'socialites' and radio 'personalities'. While waiting for the right critic to knock on our door, we all had a go, especially Clyde Packer (who called himself Johnny, as at the stage door, and concentrated on musicals) and Michael Baume (who preferred to be Ramsay Pennicuick, at the opera.)

My own best effort (under my real name) went into a critique of the Barry Humphries–Peter O'Shaughnessy production of

Samuel Beckett's *Waiting for Godot*—its Australian premiere. The two actors were at the high point of their five-year partnership, a short but historic collaboration that saw their children's play *The Bunyip and the Satellite*, the revue *Rock 'n Reel*, and the Dada Laurel and Hardy show *Waiting for Godot*. The public was overwhelmingly indifferent to *Godot*. About fifteen devotees turned up each night in Sydney—an attendance not increased by the actors' practice, at least partly contemptuous, of baiting the audience by prolonging the silences unendurably, each sigh or groan from the stalls a triumph . . . I remained a sceptic and wrote in my review:

> *Waiting for Godot* is about the Human Predicament and all that jazz . . . Everything about this production is good except the play. Beckett makes his point very well in the first act, and the second act adds nothing whatsoever except tedium. The philistines are right again: the play, or rather the second act, is a hoax.

A bit brash, although I still haven't changed my view entirely. But I might have congratulated them on the hoax and urged people to rush off and see the first act. Humphries told me later that *Godot* had changed his life.

We invited the two actors home for dinner, Humphries sitting with an air of exasperated silence, O'Shaughnessy of pained patience. As we opened the next bottle of wine, O'Shaughnessy finally leaned forward: 'Tell me, Peter, *when* were the philistines *ever* right?' 'Yes!' said Humphries warming his hands at the faggots. 'An explanation is, I believe, called . . .' He coughed, and added '. . . for'.

I had no urge to defend the philistines, only to note that men of culture may also make fools of themselves. O'Shaughnessy was unimpressed. Disdainfully curling his lips, he asked his next question: 'Peter, what *is* the Human Predicament and *all that jazz*?'

The argument fizzled out when O'Shaughnessy agreed to write a Letter to the Editor. The play, his letter explained, deals with man's inability to adjust the pleasure principle in his private life to his social 'duty'; with the recurrence of a 'father image' even to those who have rejected God through rational argument; and with the way we turn a blind eye to many injustices . . . Spain, Hungary, Cyprus . . . 'These themes are painful ones . . .' Humphries' more effective rejoinder came a little later when he created a nose-picking, toe-picking beatnik guitarist called Pete who crooned: 'I really get sick of, like nobody has / The Human Predicament *and all that jazz*'.

I was able to persuade Humphries to write for us occasionally. He brought a welcome and anarchic freethought to our theatre pages, but it was an uneasy arrangement. He is not by nature—or was not then—a newspaper or magazine critic, ready to meet deadlines, writing to an agreed length, accepting cuts and 'rewrites'. It is a genre he enjoyed parodying.

He gave us one memorable piece ridiculing the Elizabethan Theatre Trust's namby-pamby Melbourne production of the new musical *Lola Montez*. When I rewrote some of its idiosyncratic paragraphs 'to style', he accepted this editing with a shrug (and sent me a copy of Richard Garnett's *Twilight of the Gods*, written in the sort of mannered style that he then enjoyed).

It was a good stroke to put on record in the *Observer* Humphries' criticism of the Australian stage at that formative period of his (and its) career—although the edited article lost some of the eccentric intensity of the original. Humphries, the Dada Dandy, did not write this piece. He had not yet fully emerged. But its savage realism and contempt for theatrical phoniness were already at the heart of his work. He used the device of taking Henry Handel Richardson's Ballarat in *The Fortunes of Richard Mahony*, with its bullock teams, pack horses, thieves, bushrangers, convicts, expirees, Chinese, Lascars, Turks and Jews, and contrasting it with the Ballarat of the fugitives from *Paint Your Wagon* on the stage in Melbourne:

> The most depressing feature of this production was its aggressively hygienic atmosphere: the settings were clean and claustrophobic,

the actors never being permitted to escape into reality; a semi-balletic scene on the goldfields was conducted behind a gauze screen, to protect the audience from an unpleasant awareness of sweat and toil—a jolly song 'There's Gold in Them Thar Hills' accompanying this decorative tableau . . .

His criticism had some influence on the less sanitised Sydney production, and the article remains unique in Humphries' oeuvre.

Our next step into Australian drama was the recruitment of Ray Mathew. If Bob Hughes and Bruce Beresford knocked on our door, we knocked on Ray Mathew's, almost by accident. Donald Horne's friend, Myfanwy Gollan (whom he was soon to marry) took him one Sunday night to a reading of a new play by Mathew at Doris Fitton's Independent Theatre. Horne went unwillingly, expecting a night of heavy clichés in pretentious language. Ray Lawler's *Doll* was changing the public's expectation, but Australian plays on the whole were still bad news.

The play was *The Life of the Party*. Set in Kings Cross, it was about drunks, bohemians, homosexuals and wife-swappers. Horne loved it. 'There are,' he wrote in the next *Observer*, 'two off-stage seductions and two off-stage suicides, but none of this is to be taken too seriously.' The play's 'astringent charm' lay in 'the endless, nervous, verbal fretting about love, sex and marriage'. *The Life* (Horne went on) had nothing new to say but said things, wittily, that were not usually spoken aloud. It was one of the first Australian plays that could be called sophisticated. You could put it on in Paris tomorrow. The comparison with Anouilh's *Waltz of the Toreadors* was inevitable. But it hadn't a hope in Sydney—given the hopelessness of both the subsidised Elizabethan Theatre Trust and the private enterprise of J. C. Williamson.

Ray Mathew, a slight young man not yet 30, amused, elusive, argumentative, of gentle manner and wicked wit, insisted he could not live up to this image of the Parisian boulevardier. 'You have invented me, Donald,' he complained, like a character in his plays.

He was one of the last major writers to be obsessed with the issue of what it means to be an Australian—an antipodean, an exile. When he spoke, for example, of 'the Australian language', he did not mean its words or idioms but its nuances. He found an *Australian truth* (drawling avoidance of emotion) in Gordon Parsons' song 'The Pub with No Beer' and noted the *foreigner's eye* (that is, a New Zealander's) in Douglas Stewart's vision of Australian landscape.

He had made his name with *A Spring Song*, which will always remain in the repertoire of Australian little theatres, and it was in his examination of the little theatres and their policies that Ray Mathew made his main contribution to the *Observer*'s coverage.

He was a loner among *Observer* writers, with his leftist contempt for the magazine's 'radical conservatism'. He also ridiculed Jim McAuley's censorious 'race of poet-men':

> The callous ecstasy of Greece
> In them has found a Christian peace.

(McAuley shrugged: 'Ray says we write metrically, are unpleasantly religious, and won't fornicate like the ancient Greeks. I can't comment on all that.') But he was a useful reviewer of the books by Australian leftists—say Vance Palmer or K. S. Prichard or Dorothy Hewett—always being at once critical and sympathetic.

About this time I published a *Current Affairs Bulletin* on the work of D. H. Lawrence—a silly essay that I should not like to see reprinted under any circumstances. I was in those days preoccupied with Lawrence, his ideas of men and women, and his related critique of what we would now call consumerism and economic development. The *CAB* got a lot of it out of my system.

Since Mathew assured me I had got Lawrence all wrong, it seemed sensible to ask him to review my *CAB* for the *Observer* and in a few words he said all that was needed: '. . . the basic point is that Lawrence did not like women . . . He is curiously like Henry Lawson. His good women are *mates*.' The extraordinary thing, Mathew concluded, is that he makes this seem 'incredibly desirable'.

Since our association with Mathew began with Horne's discovery of *The Life of the Party*, we followed the play through to the end. Like Hughes and Humphries, Mathew soon went abroad, in his case to keep an eye on the London production of *The Life of the Party*. It was a nightmare. The London director thoroughly 'revised' the play: 'I love your oblique writing, but most of the audience will be 14-year-old readers of the *Daily Whatsit*.' After a year of revisions, arguments, rehearsals and appeals to the Lord Chamberlain, it finally opened and was a flop. The critics were merciless.

Mathew never returned to Australia and now lives in Manhattan. The London experience tempered, if it did not finish off, his Australianism. In any case he has not published since.

Kevon Kemp, a producer, finally took his place on our drama critic's perch in Sydney, assisted by Madeleine Armstrong in Melbourne, both joining a battery of *Observer* irregulars who filled the aching gaps in Australian journalism. Adrian Rawlins blew in from Cootamundra to report on the jazz festival. Alan Brissenden covered ballet. Chris Wallace-Crabbe kept a poet's eye, and John Brack a painter's, on Melbourne art. Bob Raymond became Australia's first critic of the press, writing under the name Autolycus, which he took from his old London circle in the *New Statesman*. Heinz Arndt became a correspondent on Asian economic affairs, a preoccupation that culminated in his Centre for Asian Studies in Canberra. Len Evans, at the time a glass-washer at the Ship Inn (now demolished) and not yet a cellar-master, gave us sketches of life in the public bar. (In due course we trained him to write about wine!)

John Croyston, under the name John Holdaway, became the first independent television critic (which brought out one of the limitations on our freedom, since Frank Packer who owned the *Observer* was also the licensee of Channel 9 and insisted that critics whom he paid be 'objective *our way!*' Croyston was simply objective.) Francis James became our ecclesiastical correspondent, beginning with 'How to be a Bishop', his liberal spoof of the Anglican Church's weakness for English archbishops. Canonical fitness, he wrote, is less important than shape of calf (condign, never spindly) or quality of voice (always conveying, whether the occasion be sad or gay, a sense of faint regret at something or other).

David Stove, a freethinker of corrosive integrity and one of Australia's finest essayists, was our university correspondent and adviser, although his first piece, condemning the new spirit of greed and trade unionism among academics, left him with few followers in or out of academia.

One of our most popular irregulars was Myfanwy Gollan, who became Australia's first consumerist critic, elegantly complaining about the quality of goods and services. The advent of the supermarket provided her with a rich field, but one of her most telling pieces, to judge by the public response, was a critique of dry-cleaners. At the very time when John F. Kennedy defeated Richard Nixon to become the first Roman Catholic President of the USA and his New Frontier was being inaugurated around the world, we received far more phone calls and letters on the following drama:

> A few years ago I had to have a long evening dress dry-cleaned in a hurry. I needed it for a reporting job, one of those rare occasions when a short dress would have been out of place. My usual dry-cleaner was away. I went to another . . . a simple enough job, a couple of spots to be removed from pale blue taffeta. But the next day it was not ready, and the next day I refused to accept it as it looked worse than it had beforehand. The dress had to be flown to me inter-State and when it arrived it looked even worse: the taffeta was limp and thin. The dry-cleaning firm went down on my list of firms I would never patronise again.

But the next dry-cleaner was also a disaster: it lost a belt buckle off a dress and broke the clasp of a handbag. 'That will be 7/6, please,' said the woman behind the counter.

> The point is both these shops are, as I discovered in my fury, not

competitors but allies. The articles delivered to both are cleaned in the same factory. It is wise to find out just where the work you give to the little shop on the corner is done . . .

That same week South Africa severed its ties with the monarchy to become an apartheid Republic, but what people wanted to talk about was the buckles their dry-cleaners had lost. Myfanwy Gollan's columns did more than their share to fuel the drive to consumer protection.

But the groping, searching or ironic mood of our critics was probably best caught by our cartoonist Les Tanner, who moved into the *Observer* circle when Bob Hughes left for London. Unlike other contributors, Tanner had grown up in publishing, in the cock-snooting, drunken, gambling, rorty era caught in the tales of Lennie Lower. I felt I had known him for years. My first brush with his family was in my student days in the late 1940s when you could get well-paid but exhausting work on Saturday nights loading heavy bundles of the Sunday paper on to delivery trucks. After a few hours of this yakka, you might be able to catch your breath by slipping into one of the toilet cubicles for a moment or two. But Tanner's father, who was by then one of the senior hands, would march up and down banging on the doors shouting: 'Come on, you dry shitters! Back to the dock!'

Tanner worked as a copy boy on the *Daily Telegraph* until the legendary editor Brian Penton sacked Finey and Mahony when they refused to do cartoons ridiculing the Communist Party during a 1944 strike. They moved to the communist-controlled journalists' newspaper, but as a mere copy boy, Tanner stayed on and found himself drawing dinkuses and jokes. ('Pinch a caption from *Punch*,' he was told, 'and draw it like the *New Yorker*!') When the strike ended, he still avoided cartooning because it would conflict with his communist principles. The Soviet suppression of Hungary in 1956 liberated him from these fixations and he gradually began doing cartoons. It was still a declining wasteland. *Smith's Weekly* had gone. The *Bulletin*'s great days were past. Cartooning had become a matter of grinding out facetious cracks at this funny old world. But Molnar remained a beacon.

Tanner knew the history of Australian black-and-white, the high and low points. He and I did a book together—*Cartoons of Australian History*—and it led him on to a study of our first mordant cartoonist, William Lushington Goodwin of the *Cornwall Chronicle* in Van Diemen's Land. He now wanted to revive this mordant tradition, and in the *Observer* he found the eager editorial collaboration he knew was essential to effective cartooning. (He used to refer to the *Sydney Morning Herald* cartoonist who signed his work Kurt Nodt: the only acknowledgement he ever received from the editor was a curt nod.)

The period was made for Tanner. It was the cusp of the 1960s, with everything in flux—the time of JFK, Castro, Sharpeville, Winds of Change, the last writhings of angry young men and the first crackers of the satire boom in Swinging England. The folk song revival, the beginnings of multiculturalism, the stirrings of republicanism and the great art explosion were further grist to his mill of fortnightly cartoons and jokes. He also designed covers around his caricatures of the great figures of the day—from Doc Evatt and Arthur Calwell to Vince Gair or Bob Hawke, but above all Bob Menzies, the eternal Prime Minister, the personification of the days 'When the Going was Good'.

The *Observer* struggled to find form as a literary magazine—a forum for poets and novelists as well as critics. We published established poets—Ray Mathew, Geoffrey Dutton, John Croyston, Lex Banning (including his 'Romancero') and James McAuley (including 'The Inception' of *Captain Quiros*)—and a few who were new and unknown, especially Barbara Fisher who gave us a poem of the now forgotten Phillip Street where I had lived as a student. Called 'Demolished Residential', it moved me deeply as a glimpse of a lost world:

Yesterday in Phillip Street I saw
Fireplaces six hung on a wall,
Sockets of some private lives
Concluding very small.

Mr Carruthers went to relations,
Giving up sardines and tea
For the regular meals of his sister's
Trim household in Willoughby.

Mr McClosky suddenly woke—
His bed was moving with light.
The Railway Hotel gave a shudder,
The train passed into the night.

Fat Mrs Cruse and her shivering dog
Found sanctuary in a tram,
Marooned in somebody's paddock
With a present of melon jam.

Mr Roscorla was put in a home,
Where he sat in a sea-grass chair
Looking all day at the ocean
And wondering why he was there.

Mr Dinwiddy of butterfly collar
Found board in Neutral Bay.
Dinners were not undertaken;
Cornflakes came in on a tray.

But Miss Annie Agnew, pamphleteer,
Was far too busy to care;
She could write letters to papers,
Be angry, anywhere.

Barbara Fisher came, as it were, into our lives, published a few memorable lyrics, and then disappeared. As far as I can tell she never published again, at least under that name.

One of our most resonant literary controversies—the Banning–Croyston affair—was a result of my reckless shortening, in the rush on production day, of the title of a poem to make it fit the space. Lex Banning had given me a poem called 'Being a Variation on a Theme by John Croyston', which I foolishly shortened to 'John Croyston'. It read:

> Poor Poetry, they said,
> poor poetry is fled
> and gone to his death-bed.
>
> They said, and I concurred
> until your voice I heard
> and knew that I had erred,
>
> reading in your eyes
> those words unto the wise
> that 'beauty never dies'.
>
> How vain had been our weeping,
> for safely in your keeping
> had Poetry been sleeping.

In the following issue Banning published a letter complaining about the unauthorised alteration which left the poem open, he said, to 'disagreeable and even peculiar interpretations'. We apologised but meanwhile Croyston had sent in his 'Variation on a Theme by Lex Banning':

> Oh, thou art food for poets,
> Brave Poetry,

> On which the poets feed,
> But poorly.
>
> Truly, not thou,
> But the Poet sleeps,
> And not the Poet
> But the Public weeps.
>
> And cruel Justice,
> In reverse,
> Puts the Thinness
> In their verse.

Banning replied:

> I see John Croyston, being terse,
> Imputes a 'thinness' to my verse.
> I wonder, could it elsewise seem,
> Remembering whence I took my theme?
>
> The food of poets, sir, of course,
> Is much influenced by its source;
> Though Poetry feed poets all,
> Poor John must yet turn cannibal.

Richard Appleton (who many years later edited a selection of Lex Banning's verse) thereupon submitted his 'Being a Variation on a Theme by John Croyston, by Lex Banning, and a Variation on a Theme by Lex Banning, by John Croyston . . . A Variation:

> Ring thy change for charity,
> A brace of muses passeth by
> Bedevilled by their bards' dispute,
> Thus unemployed . . . and destitute.

Croyston ended the exchange:

> Sir,
> Poor Lex Banning, thin he is,
> Involved in these complexities;
> Worried still about his food,
> He versifies in hungry mood.
>
> And fearing for the simpletons
> Not immobile as Appletons
> Another voice has passed the time
> By indigesting in his rhyme.
>
> But let me practise charity
> And force 'An Instant's Clarity',
> Knowing all are overdosed,
> Declare the correspondence closed.

After all this I adopted the practice of sending Banning a proof of any future contributions with a note: 'Is this alright?'

The *Observer* was never able to find a place for fiction or short stories. We had no theory about this. We knew instinctively that the conventional short story increasingly lacked the bite or immediacy we were looking for. But we struck a rich vein in memoirs which helped develop our preoccupation with the passing of the old Australia and the advent of something still obscure.

These memoirs were usually on the theme 'When I was Kid', always short and often deeply moving—such as Thelma Forshaw's account of her emergence as a writer at her convent and the suppression of her impulse to draw or paint; or Sheila Patrick's sketch of her schoolgirl flirtation during the war with a Dutch sailor—holding hands on the ferry, mooning about the Botanical Gardens, learning Dutch songs. (He 'sailed away . . . and didn't come back to me . . . I've forgiven him . . . I'll never forget him.')

Gwen Kelly (on the Commonwealth Public Service in the war), Ailsa Burns (Toorak during the Depression and the infantile paralysis epidemic), Douglas Terry (on Springwood in the 1930s), Bernard Hesling (on the bohemian club Pakie's, now demolished) and Hugh Atkinson (on Buggery Barn, the artists' colony, also demolished) were other memoirists of the way of life that was disappearing before our eyes as surely as the residentials of Barbara Fisher's poem.

Several of these writers used the sketches as first drafts which they would later develop into major stories. Hugh Atkinson wrote several, beginning with 'My Two White Feathers' about his long effort, while in prison early in the war, to have himself classified as 'a war resister' rather than as a conscientious objector: he had no objection at all to fighting, only to fighting the war in 1939. (When at last a baffled magistrate found some formula for him, Atkinson put the piece of paper away and volunteered for combatant service with the RAAF, in which he was awarded a Distinguished Flying Cross.) A good deal of the yarn reappeared in his novel of bohemian life, *Low Company*. His longest sketch was 'Murdered Valley', which turned up 30 years later as his masterly novel *Grey's Valley*. Bob Raymond's memoir of his spell in the London blitz, which helped Eric Baume invent sensational war news for Ezra Norton's new *Daily Mirror* ('Tin Hats at the Savoy'), also turned up 30 years later in his autobiography, *From Bees to Buzz-Bombs*.

Our involvement in the arts seemed to lead naturally to literary politics. Of the uncounted articles I wrote under all sorts of pseudonyms, the one that has been the most quoted (next to a sketch of young Robert James Lee Hawke) was one called 'Literary Gangs at War'.

It looked back at Ern Malley and suggested that Max Harris, a poet of great flair, would not lack champions in the future. It also noted the conspiracy of silence against McAuley's *Quadrant* (citing, for example, Ray Mathew's recent *Current Affairs Bulletin* which managed to refer to every literary magazine except *Quadrant*) and asked why the Commonwealth Literary Fund was subsidising *Meanjin* and *Southerly* but not *Quadrant*. But the campaign against *Quadrant* was, I conceded, mild indeed when compared with the communist campaign against the ex-communist *Overland*: its writers were accused of McCarthyism, pornography, drunkenness, homosexuality, embezzling, police-informing, even flirting with Christianity. I also saw fit to suggest that these efforts presaged a subtler gang warfare in the coming years, when reputations would be routinely demolished and works suppressed in the name of a new Australian orthodoxy, often backed by the arts bureaucracy . . .

CHAPTER 9
Cold War

What are the chief evils of Australian life? asked Vincent Buckley in *Prospect*, a liberal Catholic magazine he edited with Paul Simpson. His answer was swift: humbug, provincialism, quietism, conservatism, cynicism, self-righteousness, stereotypical thinking, ignorance of totalitarianism, and debasement of the idea of God! But all was not lost, Buckley added: the *Observer*, at least, was tackling these issues 'in a forthright and sensible way'.

Our ambitions were high, even astounding . . . but *that* high? *that* astounding? We were still beginners, uncertain, feeling our way, seeking a new consensus neither traditionalist nor radical. But Buckley's summary—after two years of fortnightly publication—helped us feel we were getting somewhere.

The Orr case was our synecdoche for Australia—the eccentric individualist victimised by mean and unimaginative conservatives. If this meant we sometimes championed a few cranks and their causes, we also took the side of Frank Knöpfelmacher versus fuddy-duddy professors; Russel Ward versus a servile academic administration; Max Gluckman versus ignorant officials; Peter Clyne versus reactionary lawyers . . . We called for the abolition of censorship, the freeing up of divorce, a new deal for women, the acknowledgement of ethnic diversity, the advancement of Aborigines, and rights for prisoners . . . We were swimming with the tide, but a little faster than most.

The *Observer* was the first Australian magazine to advocate the reform of the laws governing homosexuals. In an early issue the sociologist Morven Brown called for more 'civilised' legislation, deplored public hostility to homosexuals 'out of all proportion to the social nuisance', and criticised the British Wolfenden Report on homosexual offences and prostitution for its liberal 'hangovers of revulsion stemming from hoary tradition'.

The psychologist Frank Knöpfelmacher condemned the existing law as 'not in the public interest' (benefiting only blackmailers and spies). Another psychologist, John Maze, saw everyone as more or less bisexual: 'Whether one is as square as a butter box or as camp as a row of tents, the underlying mixture is much the same'.

For Henry Mayer, this was all liberal mush! To hell with adjustment and deviations! he would shout—and then ask obscurely: Who holds the levers? *That* is the question. His answer was not quite inscrutable: 'It's the power structure!' But he too was a reformer, or rather a liberationist *avant la lettre*.

I found myself under censure by the Anglican Bishop of Adelaide over a report I prepared on the plight of part-Aborigines, the *Fringe Dwellers* of Bruce Beresford's film and Nene Gare's novel. The report contained these snotty lines:

> . . . But their life is still embittering. Hollow men who ape conventions they do not understand, they are never quite sure how to behave, always feeling there is something new to learn about social life—perhaps from a book, a film, an overheard conversation . . .

Was I describing myself in code? In any case I went on:

> They are insecure, reserved, self-conscious. They are often snubbed and daily come up against irritating petty prejudices. It may be an Anglican priest who does not want them at communion sipping wine from the same cup as the whites . . .

The Bishop of Adelaide wrote us a letter: 'I wish to protest against the gratuitous insult to the Church of England . . . In all my experience as a clergyman during the past 33 years I have never seen or heard of such a thing happening . . .' He then went further:

> Unless the writer of the article can produce evidence of such a thing happening, by giving the date, place, and name of the clergyman concerned, he should publish in your paper an apology.

He signed the letter Thomas Adelaide, Bishop's Court. I had not met him, although I had heard of him (T. T. Reed) as a respected literary critic and authority on Henry Kendall. But the tone of his letter shook me. I did not want to be taken as ignoring the Church's work among Aborigines, let alone offering it a 'gratuitous insult'. Nor did I want to 'name names' of particular clergymen with whom I had discussed the matter. Fortunately I had no trouble citing published academic research supporting my article (while stressing that discrimination was exceptional). But it was the most serious criticism I had received since joining the *Observer* and an experience not quickly forgotten. It is not every day that you are condemned, unfairly, by a bishop.

But literary censorship, one of the *Observer*'s favourite crusades, was my main bag. Apart from covering the various cases and controversies, we had two lines of policy. We were against the mindless calls for national unity in censorship: different communities and States had differing attitudes; there is value in diversity and experiment; and there is danger in centralised control. We also liked to tell readers (and writers) to stop bellyaching about censors and start challenging them in court. We had a friend of sorts in the then Minister for Customs, Senator Henty, whom I met when writing my book *Obscenity Blasphemy Sedition*. He was the first of the moderate reformers. Writers, he thought, were nuisances and a bit peculiar at the best of times, but they should be kept as happy as possible. He only drew the line when they began encouraging appalling vices. The trouble was that so many of the major books of the day seemed to him to do just that—

Lolita (paedophilia), *Borstal Boy* (bestiality), *Lady Chatterley's Lover* (buggery).

In the case of Lady Chatterley, he banned not only Lawrence's novel but C. H. Rolph's account of the English obscenity case, *The Trial of Lady Chatterley*. I immediately wrote a book for the Sydney publisher Horwitz, called *The Case of Lady Chatterley's Lover*, which drew on the detailed reports of the case in the London press and which, as a local and not an imported book, was outside any Customs prohibition and could be sold freely (unless the State authorities banned it, and none was silly enough to try). It all helped to make the Commonwealth look ridiculous.

In politics we roamed the world from Johannesburg and Madrid to Dublin and Little Rock offering our liberal advice. But inevitably the Cold War was the great theme—the oppression of millions by communist governments and the prestige these governments still enjoyed.

Dick Spann from Manchester, who was at once liberal and conservative, laid down the ground rules for debating these issues in a civil way. It was not always easy. The arguments quickly became emotional. The *Observer* began operations in the period between the Soviet suppression of the Hungarian Revolution and the ascension of Fidel Castro in Havana. Soon after our first issue, the Soviet authorities, including its servile Writers' Union, began harassing Boris Pasternak for writing *Dr Zhivago*.

We drew our ideas and commentators from three sources—old freethinkers, former Marxists, ex-Trotskyists ranging from Douglas McCallum to Laurie Short; Central European refugees from Hitler or Stalin who understood the twentieth century, particularly Henry Mayer, Frank Knöpfelmacher, Eugene Kamenka and Hugo Wolfsohn; and Catholics of the Pope Paul formation, especially Jim McAuley, whose politics were an amalgam of John Anderson and Bob Santamaria in their Sorelian modes. Owen Harries, now the editor of *The National Interest* in Washington, DC, was the creative misfit who eluded these categories.

We began calmly—with McCallum assessing the rise of

Khrushchev and Short calling for secret ballots in union elections. But tempers soon frayed. In May 1958, as decolonisation gained pace in Africa, McAuley called for decolonisation of the Soviet empire and referred to Australia's 'frightening security problem'. This brought in H. W. Arndt, who in turn brought in Frank Knöpfelmacher—both from Central Europe and apparently incompatible.

Heinz Arndt had grown up in Weimar Germany and moved to England with his family after the Nazis had dismissed his father from his Chair in Hamburg under the Aryan Laws. Interned as an enemy alien when the war began, Arndt continued to support the Hitler–Stalin pact and the Communist Party's opposition to the 'imperialist war' against Hitler—although only after days of embittered argument with his fellow internees on the Isle of Man. When released, he found he could no longer stomach the Communist Party's continuing anti-war line. But the memory of having swallowed it at all was a permanent reminder of the dangers of ideology. 'I felt ashamed,' he said later. 'I had surrendered my intellectual integrity.' Arthur Koestler's *Darkness at Noon* clarified the process of intellectual self-destruction and 'cured me'.

Arriving in Sydney in 1946, he was for some 15 years—including his *Observer* period—a social democratic influence in the Labor Party (finally breaking with it later over Vietnam policy). He was also a liberal and civil influence in public life at large.

Partly goaded by McAuley's broadsides against the Labor Party's foreign policy and partly by distaste for his catastrophism, Arndt warned him in the *Observer* against reckless 'flirting with the anti-Christ'. But, unexpectedly, he also warned him against associating with 'the egregious Mr Knöpfelmacher' and such 'professional anti-communists' who have 'never understood the principles or absorbed the spirit of liberal democracy'. As it happened McAuley had not mentioned Knöpfelmacher (who had however been writing elsewhere on related themes). But Knöpfelmacher seized the chance to intervene and offer some observations about Arndt.

Frank (or Franta) Knöpfelmacher grew up in Moravia in a

German-speaking Jewish family which was almost bankrupted during the Depression. Another turning point, which further deepened his sense of the fragility of institutions, was an exhibition in Brno (organised by Arthur Koestler and Willi Muenzenberg and partly based on faked material) of Fascist atrocities in Spain—mangled babies, disembowelled soldiers . . . It gave him a feeling of violence and death which never left him.

When the Nazis occupied Czechoslovakia he emigrated to Palestine, where he joined the Communist Party and later the Czechoslovak Army. In England he discovered George Orwell and in Normandy during the invasion of France he too read Koestler's *Darkness at Noon*: 'all my [pro-Soviet] beliefs were shattered'. But his new anti-communism only became 'emotional' in post-war Prague as he observed the communist take-over and the show-trials in Eastern Europe. (The bestial Stalinist treatment of Kostov, the Bulgarian Jewish communist hunchback, was decisive.) He returned to England in 1948 and came to Australia in 1955—a doctor learned in comparative totalitarianism.

He was, he wrote in the *Observer*, a liberal follower of the Austrians Schumpeter and Popper and of the Englishman J. S. Mill. Then warming as to a feud: 'It would appear that liberal spirit must have been abundant in Breslau where he [Arndt] comes from and scarce in Prague where I come from . . .' (Breslau—now Wroclaw—was then German if not Nazi, and Prague Czech if not anti-Nazi.) But a free society must be defended against both totalitarians *and* 'unworthy' liberals [Arndt?] who resort to 'smear and calumny'.

At this point Dick Spann wrote his brief *Ethics of Controversy*. Brought up a Tory in Manchester, his schooling turned him into a liberal, although the Toryism kept popping up. The secret aim of liberals, he once told me, is to make the rest of us feel morally inferior, and the really nice people you meet tend to be inarticulate, shrewd and apt to have to do other people's dirty work. In earlier years in Manchester he had acted, he recalled, as a sort of chauffeur for the intellectuals and philosophers of the Congress

for Cultural Freedom on their anti-communist lecture tours—
Hannah Arendt, Raymond Aron, Bertrand de Jouvenel . . . They
were, he said, 'even more helpless in practical affairs than I'.

In the present disordered world, he wrote in the *Observer*,

> many more-or-less honest people (as well as a good many more-or-less dishonest ones) are deeply divided on some major issues of policy. That is all the more reason why they should recognise one another as tolerably honest opponents, open to conviction by the truth as they can be made to see it.
>
> We should not renounce this belief in one another's credentials till we are inescapably driven to do so.
>
> There are stupid, cowardly, opportunistic 'intellectuals'. There are also plenty of unpleasant fanatics, power-worshippers, power-seekers around. No doubt we are all, to some point, affected by one or other of these characteristics.
>
> But is it a completely feeble and pompous thing to ask those of us who are proud of being 'committed' in this way or that, if some, at least, of our enemies are not friends in disguise, who could teach us something if we cared to learn it? And to whom we might also teach something if we could resist the temptation to hurt and rebuff them?
>
> Very wishy-washy stuff; though certainly not intended to inhibit the interchange of knockdown arguments, as long as they are arguments; or even of abuse, but not knockdown abuse.

We forthwith adopted Spann's principles, although it was not always a simple matter to conform to them. We also applied them to literary debates. If a novel by a communist came out, I would get Ray Mathew to review it to ensure it was treated on its literary merits and not denounced simply because of its author's nutty politics. When an anti-communist novel such as Tibor Meray's *The Enemy* came out, we would get Lex Banning to review for similar reasons.

Henry Mayer especially welcomed the Spann rules. He was one

of the '*Dunera* boys', the internees who arrived in Australia in September 1940. A scholarly bohemian, he boasted that he had earned his living in London as publicity officer for a Soho jazzband, before being, like Arndt, interned as an enemy alien. He wrote a number of lousy poems about his ordeal on the *Dunera* of which this credo has the best lines:

> A chancy sudden death
> Must be preferred
> To atrophy of limb after limb

The Australians at detention centres were, he said, repulsive, stupid, ignorant, parochial and anti-semitic. 'Just like,' he added, poker-faced, 'everyone everywhere.'

Committed with great passion to passionless objectivity, he believed that joining any political movement meant losing all intellectual integrity. One of the rare times I saw him silenced, however briefly, was at a meeting in the old tumbledown rooms of *Quadrant* in Albert Street when he put that view to Hal Wootten, then something of a Savonarola of anti-communism. Wootten retorted that, on the contrary, it was only by serious and sustained involvement, and sometimes disenchantment, that one learned anything at all, including the capacity to observe objectively. After a long pause, Mayer replied brightly: 'Cheer up!'

Always a Weimar intellectual, he spent as much time contemplating Hitlerism as Stalinism, always scorning the idea that these movements were somehow freakish or abnormal. They were, he insisted, all-too-normal. History is genocide. But if he accepted Hannah Arendt's identification of Nazism and communism as two variants of totalitarianism, he did so reluctantly. His heart was never anti-communist and he was most at ease pillorying conservative pieties. It was he who encouraged, and helped, me to write my first book (on censorship), and he promoted the leading academic proponents of homosexual liberationism or radical feminism. He might sometimes defend conservatism for the sake of a good argument, and even, once or twice, the Christian Church against philistine rationalists. Yet he never wrote on these issues. Until the end he had an amazing knack of holding the trust of the young, as was evidenced in the many moving tributes at his memorial service in 1991.

But the Cold War was not only a matter of doctrines or armies. This was also a new age of cultural diplomacy, of 'exchanges' among artists, writers and intellectuals. The Australian record, set by fellow-travellers and naive businessmen, had been atrocious. Would that now change with détente? Michael Lindsay, who advised us on China and had himself in his time put in a couple of years with Mao Tse-tung in Yenan, thought it unlikely. Manning Clark was the most celebrated of the Australians who made the Russian tour and his book, Meeting Soviet Man, was an important event. Jim McAuley's review in Quadrant was charitable or perhaps expedient. (He still believed it might be possible to rescue Clark from the fellow-travellers or even win him over to the Church.)

But Donald Horne in the Observer could barely contain his distaste. The book, he wrote in a memorable polemic, is marked by 'its pretension, confusion, vulgarity and downright naivete', even 'idiocy'. It was, he said 'a flop . . . disgraceful . . . outrageous'. Clark, as was his practice, did not reply.

No sooner had this review appeared than we heard the news that Alexei Surkov of the Writers' Union in Moscow was coming to Australia as a guest of the Fellowship of Australian Writers! This was too much even for the left. Patrick White found the invitation 'strange and deplorable'. Kylie Tennant said: 'Don't ask me to meet him!'

The *Observer* could not get an interview with Surkov. (He would give us an appointment and, when he did not turn up, explain that he had lost his appointment book.) But I went to hear him in the old rooms of the Fellowship of Australian Writers in Clarence Street (now an office block). Frank Hardy in one of his less glorious performances was the master of ceremonies.

Surkov projected the image of a stocky, jovial scout master in horn-rimmed spectacles. I asked him why he had gone to Italy to persuade Feltrinelli not to publish *Dr Zhivago*. Pasternak, he said, was a blasphemer: he had insulted the Revolution of 1917! Nominating him for the Nobel Prize was a political stunt, he added, and his sponsors had not even read *Dr Zhivago*. (The nomination had been for his poetry.) Surkov was a perfect Writers' Union philistine with no interest in literature.

But the real pressure on Spann's rules for controversy came at the end of 1959 with the Melbourne Peace Conference—the communist attempt to regain ground lost in public opinion when Soviet forces suppressed the Hungarian bid for freedom in 1956. It was to be a great national event, with an impressive list of sponsors and several famous visitors including the English writers J. B. Priestley and his wife Jacquetta Hawkes, and the Indian novelist Mulk Raj Anand.

But the Hungarian Revolution was not to be so easily pushed to one side. 'The summer air,' as one visitor from Budapest noted, 'was thick with distrust and suspicion.' On the left, the *Overland* group—Stephen Murray-Smith, Ken Gott, David Martin—who had once defended the USSR, now drew the line. Linked with them were liberal Catholics of the *Prospect* circle, social democratic members of the Labor Party, and the *Quadrant* constituency. The *Observer's* role was to provide a forum for all these groups.

Despite these critics, a large public was still impressed by J. B. Priestley's support of the Congress—the same public that the *Observer* reached. He was a celebrated writer, novelist, playwright, critic and commentator. Jim McAuley had a soft spot for him. In a famous article in the *New Statesman*, Priestley had likened modern literature in its decline to the Mock Turtle's four branches of arithmetic—Ambition, Distraction, Uglification and Derision. Then in *Literature and Western Man* he came to the conviction that the only hope for literature was a religious revival. As McAuley said: There it is, 'Jolly Jack Priestley sharing a bench with me waiting for the end of modernity and who am I to kick him in the shins because he won't see that uttering gefuffle at peace fronts is really giving in to the dehumanising, depersonalising process in the crudest possible way?'

Priestley had a bad time with the press in Australia. But he brought a lot of it on himself. 'Are you a *Catholic!?*' he asked one reporter (who had inquired about communist control of the conference.) He told one press gathering that his distrust of the Germans was so great that, far from permitting them to rearm, he would not let them have a pop gun! But he was reported as saying he would not let the Germans have 'a pot plant'!

To counter Priestley's influence, Richard Krygier, publisher of McAuley's *Quadrant*, arranged through the Congress for Cultural Freedom in Paris, for Tibor Meray to return to Australia. Meray, the ex-communist Hungarian editor, had the respect of the *Overland* circle of leftist writers, although he never had the wide public appeal of Priestley. (Krygier also arranged for Arthur Schlesinger to persuade Eleanor Roosevelt to withdraw her name as a sponsor of the conference.)

The various anti-communists, however disparate and uncooperative, were entirely successful. It was, Vincent Buckley wrote, a 'barbarous' conference with an atmosphere that made him think of life in an iron lung. When the art and literature group rejected a resolution of support for imprisoned Hungarian writers, or even a vague statement deploring writers' lack of freedom in a number of unnamed countries, Priestley and his wife Jacquetta Hawkes (and Mulk Raj Anand) finally dissociated themselves from the decision—in a blaze of publicity.

The congress was a Communist Party disaster. At a final counter-conference, the dissenters, including James Jupp and Barry Jones, documented the details of communist control and the *Observer* published their reports. They were an invaluable record that, Vincent Buckley wrote later, alone 'stood in the way of the self-justifying lies, legends and myths which had begun to run towards the pool of history'.

The matter did not stop with the communists' defeat. Buckley headed a Tibor Dery Committee and organised a letter to be sent to Budapest signed by 47 writers including Lex Banning, Bob Brissenden, Sam Goldberg, Ken Hince, Alec Hope, Donald Horne, Des O'Grady, Chris Wallace-Crabbe and me. Before we could post our letter, the Hungarian puppets released Tibor Dery and Gyula Hay. But since many less well known writers remained in prison, we still sent our letter off to Janos Kadar.

The whole affair was probably the high point of the *Observer*'s role in cultural politics. We had won the argument. But many were quick to remind us we had not won the battle. The pro-Soviet and anti-West 'peace movement' went from strength to strength.

I was preoccupied at the time with the birth of my son, but when the conference was all over, a detail that stuck in my memory was a letter from Ken Gott commenting on a jibe I had made about some 'Trotskyist priests' at the conference. Alas, he wrote, all the men of god have become Stalinists . . .

CHAPTER 10
Competitors and Allies

If Vincent Buckley was right and 1958 was 'a crucial year' for Australians, it was inevitable that the *Observer* would not be left to reflect it alone and that other magazines would compete in setting the agenda. One of the most important appeared late in 1958 when Tom Fitzgerald began publishing *Nation* as a sort of left-liberal alternative to the *Observer*.

Tom Fitzgerald—an old RAAF (Battle of Britain) navigator, a former editor of the *Bulletin*'s business review, the *Wild Cat Monthly*, and now the financial editor of the *Sydney Morning Herald*, where he was noted for his crisp, stylish and thorough exposure of swindlers—had mortgaged his Abbotsford house to raise the funds to start *Nation*. A radical liberal who admired the England of George Orwell and the America of the *New Republic*, he soon attracted a range of well known contributors—Peter Ryan, Cyril Pearl, Hugh Stretton, Maria Prerauer, Sylvia Lawson and Ken Inglis among many others—and the support of the Anglo–Catholic parish of Christ Church St Laurence whose crypt, thanks to the intervention of *Nation*'s printer, Francis James, served as the first editorial office.

But it was his coming together with George Munster that made the difference. Barry Humphries introduced Munster—in Lorenzini's Elizabeth Street wine bar (still a wine cellar but no longer a bar) where Fitzgerald and his circle gathered: 'I want you to meet a friend of mine who is a genius'.

Fitzgerald, the Irish–Australian autodidact, immediately clicked with Munster, the archetypal Jewish intellectual and Krausianer from Hitler's Vienna. Munster gladly agreed to be an editor and all-purpose fugleman of the new enterprise.

This meeting was a timely accident for Munster. The years had passed since his early fame and promise. He had not yet written his great books. He was becoming a butt of ridicule. The strain was showing. But in *Nation* he found causes, friends, wife and whatever contentment his restless spirit ever knew.

The fortnightly they produced set out to give the universal Australian stodge (as they put it in their first editorial) a bit of a stir. They wanted to loosen up and liberalise both the stuffy conservatives and the dogmatic lefties. But they were not dogmatists, socialists or fellow-travellers. They were for immigration reform (in the last days of White Australia), for reduced censorship (in its last days), for a certain cultural nationalism (in its early days) and for some scepticism about big business. Abroad they wanted more foreign aid (Fitzgerald ridiculed left-liberals who denounced South African apartheid but did nothing for the millions starving to death in Biafra) and a foreign policy that did not always look to America for leadership (while acknowledging the essential liberalism of American policies).

Nation was lively competition for the *Observer*. When the copyboy would slap each issue on my desk every other Thursday, I would nervously flip through its pages fearing they had scooped us on something or other—a business fraud, a cultural happening, a profile of one of the *pomposi* then in the news. We also lost a number of contributors to it, including Robert Hughes, who told me later that he regretted the switch because, for all its worthiness, he found *Nation* too staid, too self-righteous for his derisive wit. The *Observer*, he said, was more fun. But the difference was more than a matter of fun. *Nation* paid a price for its detachment. It never had nor wanted a conservative constituency and throughout the 1960s it increasingly lost ground to the counter-culture, to whom it had little to say. What began as a voice for small 'l' liberalism had become, as Tom Fitzgerald frankly noted, the organ of the twee. In 1972 it merged with the counter-cultural *Sunday Review*, which Fitzgerald privately despised, although Munster was able to survive the transition.

But while the Fitzgerald–Munster *Nation* was our main competitor, Jim McAuley's *Quadrant*—then a quarterly and still a new voice (the first issue was late in 1956)—was our principal ally. Its office—an old wool store (now a Japanese hotel) in Albert Street near the Quay—was already a forum for readings, launchings and seminars, and a drop-in centre for poets (from Alec Hope to Geoffrey Lehmann), painters (Jack Lynn, Stanislaus Rapotec, Nancy Short), composers (Eugene Goossens until scandal drove him out of the country), trade unionists (Laurie Short, Lloyd Ross), lawyers (John Kerr, Hal Wootten), academics (David Armstrong, Owen Harries, Dick Spann). There is nothing like it in Sydney today.

It was here that Jim McAuley and Max Harris had their first meeting many years after the Ern Malley affair. Max Harris strode in looking, in his bow tie and cane, more and more like Bunyip Bluegum in *The Magic Pudding*, while Jim McAuley was busily acting, if not looking, like Egbert Rumpus Bumpus the Poet. There was some tension as each caught the other's eye, a hush, a pause . . . Work stopped . . . Then McAuley nodded: 'Hello Max'. Harris nodded: 'Hello Jim'. Work then resumed as the two editors began discussing an article Harris was to give *Quadrant* on the achievement of *Angry Penguins*.

After hours, the office served as a meeting place for McAuley's DLP (Democratic Labor Party) friends at the time of the Labor Party splits and McAuley's frantic attempts to frustrate Dr Evatt in New South Wales. *Quadrant*'s publisher, Richard Krygier, also had a desk in one of the corners. I first met him here when I had dropped in, cheerfully eager to join his new committee for cultural freedom, only to be sent away with a flea in my ear and the intelligence that you could by no means expect to walk in off the street and be accepted into the committee! You had to be recommended! Even so, most recommendations would be rejected.

If the *Reader's Digest* had ever been foolish enough to ask me to write a piece for its series on 'The Most Remarkable Man I Have

Ever Met', I would have written about Richard Krygier. Short, egg-shaped, Jewish, irrepressible, both hard-headed and easily deceived, he was born in 1917 in Warsaw, where he had been a communist fellow-traveller until the Moscow show trials of 1938. But the truly shattering event of his youth had been the occupation of Poland by Hitler and Stalin in 1939. Making his way with his wife to Lithuania, they were among the last few to obtain visas from a philo-semitic Japanese consul who continued issuing them against his instructions from Tokyo. They then travelled across a hungry, depressed and depressing Soviet Union to Vladivostok and arrived in Sydney, via Tokyo and Shanghai, late in 1941, shortly before Pearl Harbor.

This youthful survival of both the Holocaust and the Gulag produced in Krygier a democratic, anti-totalitarian illumination that the years would only strengthen. As he once said to me: 'Between Auschwitz and Siberia, I think I prefer Sydney.'

When the Yalta agreement of 1945 led to the closing down of the Polish consulate in Sydney and the sacking of Krygier as its press officer, he set up business as a book importer. Then in June 1950, as North Korea invaded South Korea, a story in the Paris-based Polish literary journal *Kultura* caught his eye. It noted a meeting—not reported in the Australian press—of 100 intellectuals who had gathered in Berlin from around the world to debate and do something about the Cold War. They were old prisoners of Stalin's, Hitler's or Mussolini's jails, former refugees and Resistance fighters, scarred scholars, poets and artists who disagreed with each other on many issues but shared one big truth about Stalin and his gulag. They created something called the Congress for Cultural Freedom and planned more rallies and a network of magazines to oppose the Soviet cultural offensive.

Krygier wrote to the organisers in Berlin urging them to include Australia on its agenda. They ignored him, but he persisted. Finally, after almost three years, they asked him to become the Australian representative of the Congress for Cultural Freedom. In 1954—at the time of the defection of the Petrovs—he brought together a handful of notables, including the former Chief Justice of the High Court, Sir John Latham, and the composer Sir Eugene Goossens, to form an Australian committee to work for liberal causes, especially law reform (censorship, defamation, extradition), and to combat what Stephen Murray-Smith of *Overland* described as the Communist Party's 'domination' of cultural life in Australia.

But Krygier's great achievement was the founding of *Quadrant*. Its conception was in 1955 in the Russian Tea Room in West 57th Street, Manhattan, where he met with Irving Kristol, the editor of *Encounter*, to discuss the Australian situation. You should start a magazine! Kristol said. Like *Encounter!* Krygier wrote to the Paris office of the Congress for Cultural Freedom and asked for a subsidy. Malcolm Muggeridge, who had just returned from his first visit to Australia, supported Krygier and told the congress executive that this was an idea whose time had come.

Back in Australia, Bob Santamaria suggested that Jim McAuley be the editor. After meeting him, Krygier completely agreed, although some of his friends thought a Catholic convert would be useless in a secularist enterprise. But Krygier's enthusiasm carried the day. For McAuley it presented an opportunity, in literature, to promote his own post-or anti-modernist ideas of poetry and, in politics, to combat 'the colourless, odourless, tasteless, inert and neutral ideas that pass for liberalism'.

At the *Observer* I was now at last able to resume the conversation with him that we had begun at the Poetry Society a couple of years earlier before I had moved to Canberra. But I still remained baffled by the paradoxes of his extraordinary personality. He was always a mixture of the anarchist and formalist, the contemplative and the *enragé*, the dandy and the desperado.

When I began some years later to search for what I presumed to call, in the title of my book, *The Heart of James McAuley*, I was fascinated to stumble on a number of his unpublished youthful poems that expressed the same paradoxes in simpler terms. One was his rollicking 'Beer Song' of 1938:

> Oh to be in Sydney now,
> Now that I am here!
> For whoever is in Sydney now
> Is most likely drinking beer!
> (Sydney Bitter, Resch's, Foster's, Pilsener and all.
> K.B., D.A., Richmond, Double B and all!)

Another was a piece of self-hating nonsense:

> At my birth an Irish maid
> Flopped on her dirty knees and prayed:
> Avenge my insults now dear God
> And make this child a nasty sod.
>
> My parents dismissed her that same night
> But God endorsed the slavey's spite,
> And made me, as my friends admit,
> A very nasty piece of shit.

There was also among his juvenilia a foreshadowing of some of his later, more famous lyrics ('To a Dead Bird of Paradise') on the loss of the spiritual principle in our sterile life:

> I am the web in the corner
> In which the insects are caught
> But the spider lies crushed on the floor.

These moods and themes culminated in the anarchistic rhetoric of *The Blue Horses* and the nihilistic gestures of the musical *I'd Rather Be Left*. In reaction or revulsion, he turned via Ern Malley to tradition and finally to Christianity.

It was at about this stage that he became our collaborator on the *Observer*, and for me the paradoxes only deepened. One minute he was writing a tender love lyric ('Secret Song') and the next a tense hymn ('Help of Christians, guard this land'). He had also begun his great epic *Captain Quiros* and was writing the cultural critiques collected in *The End of Modernity*, which in a metropolitan culture would have been widely debated but in Australia were largely ignored.

At the same time he was obsessed with politics, especially the Labor split. He gave me a copy of his squib, in the seventeenth century style, about the Labor leader, Dr Herbert Vere Evatt—perhaps the most mordant political poem ever written in Australia:

> With daring energy and force of mind
> To some great good young Herbert seemed designed
> Which Providence for our poor country meant.
> Alas, the tree grows as the slip is bent;
> And blind ambition, twisting all awry,
> From early faults, which years but magnify,
> Produced a monster, not quite sane or mad,
> The traitors' tribune, bigots' Galahad,
> The greatest blot this country ever had.
> Through curious turns he spiralled as he grew,
> But all his windings had a lefthand screw.
> At last he rose supreme for all to see,
> The mighty Anarch of the ALP:
> More hated by his friends than by his foes—
> They praise the Leader they dare not depose.
> Now all—the fools, the knaves, the operators,
> The gelded Groupers and the Grouper-haters—
> Turned zombie by the threat of liquidation,
> Must work the bankrupt Socialist plantation.

His conversation was often savage, particularly about Sydney's Labor Party Catholics. I had to sit up in my seat once at the virulence with which he spat out his contempt for 'the little greaser', the Catholic who was at the time Premier of New South Wales, or the scorn with which he pictured one ingratiating ecclesiastic standing at the airport with a placarded smile to welcome the representatives of a conquering, atheistic regime. Another bishop, he said, confused Room 32 (then the Labor Party headquarters) with the Upper Room (of the Last Supper): 'Sometimes the cream rises to the top and sometimes the scum'. (When I later became his co-editor of *Quadrant*, I found office copies of the *Catholic Weekly* on which he had scrawled in the margins his comments on various editorials and reports. *Lies!* was his typical comment.)

He was equally withering, if more ribald, about Liberal Party politicians and officials, although in the 1950s he had less traffic with them than later. He was also, it should be remembered, broke: at the very time he was writing his great Australian and Christian epic, *Captain Quiros*, his answer to Sidney Nolan's Ned Kelly paintings, he could not meet the instalments on his Ryde council house and had to appeal to the town clerk for time to pay.

When I was trying to piece these various fragments together for *The Heart of James McAuley*, Amy Witting—McAuley's friend Joan Fraser from undergraduate days—sent me a poem for *Quadrant* simply called 'Biographical Note'. It was obviously about McAuley and seemed to me to say more about him more briefly than anything else I had read. It helped me finish my book:

> Consider an elegant house in the Japanese style,
> its paper panels meant for translucency,
> for lantern or candle-flame, then set in it
> a clamouring gang of passions, some delinquent
> and all of them too sharp-elbowed for the walls;
> also the heartless star boarder, the leech and distiller,
> the talent that knows no purpose but its own,
> and the poor tenant longing for peace and order
> and the best table in the restaurant
> with a smile form the maitre d' . . . why, he can hardly
> keep the mob quiet and keep the neighbours out.
> So he builds walls against the eyes of the world

>   and lives within a life that we cannot know,
>   and from behind them issues communiques
>   that speak to the hearts of men and will speak on
>   though the Japanese house and the fortress both are gone.

The line, 'that speak to the hearts of men and will speak on', kept ringing in my ears and I used it as the last words of my McAuley book.

His first issue of *Quadrant* came out late in 1956 and its editorial included the fine iambic lines: 'In spite of all that can be said against our age, what a moment it is to be alive in! What an epoch for a magazine to emerge in!' *Quadrant* was always far more literary than the *Observer* and we could not join McAuley in his plan to revive the epistle or the eclogue (or indeed his hope of reviving Italic handwriting). But he urged us to take particular note of Patrick White (then largely unknown and certainly undervalued in Australia) and to listen with cautious sympathy to Sydney Sparkes Orr. McAuley's obsession with the Labor Party also infected us for a time. He remained a helpful if sometimes severe collaborator.

As it turned out, the magazine with which we had our little rendezvous with destiny was not *Quadrant* but the *Bulletin*. When the *Observer* started, the *Bulletin* was still the most important literary magazine in the country, simply because it was a weekly that published more verse, fiction and criticism than any other magazine and did so promptly. With Douglas Stewart as its literary editor, supported by Ronald McCuaig, Cecil Mann, and the young John Abernethy, it was still an eager talent-spotter and brought forward new and younger poets like Ray Mathew, Lex Banning or Vivian Smith.

They had their limitations. They had little patience with the poetry of ideas—say Jim McAuley or Alec Hope—poets of the academy, as they dubbed them. They also despised F. R. Leavis and had little interest in modern thought or philosophy. Stewart preferred nature poets, and McAuley's satiric formula for an

Australian poem was largely aimed at Stewart, although it applied to many poets of the time: in Stanza 1, you identify an indigenous tree, bird or mammal; in Stanza 2, you demonstrate how well acquainted you are with it; in Stanza 3, you make it plain that the sole merit of the object is that it is an Australian object and the sole merit of the poem is that it is an Australian poem. For his part Stewart denied that he unduly favoured nature poets in the *Bulletin*. After all McCuaig never wrote a nature poem in his life.

McCuaig's has been the most neglected of all the *Bulletin* school. His *Vaudeville*—published in 1938, but written and privately printed in 1933—was an exciting new voice in Australian poetry, a potent eruption of Ezra Pound and T. S. Eliot in 1930s' Kings Cross. He joined the *Bulletin* in 1949 (publishing bleak, romantic poetry under his real name and his lighter verse by Swilliam), and took over the editing of short stories 'discovering' Hal Porter, who always spoke of his debt to McCuaig.

The *Bulletin*'s politics, heavily influenced by the historian M. H. Ellis, were paleo-conservative: nationalist, Protestant, digger, xenophobic, anti-communist and occasionally anti-semitic in the pre-Holocaust style. (During the war, it opposed the appointment of Julius Stone to the Chair of Jurisprudence on the grounds that serving soldiers could not be interviewed for the position. It ridiculed 'Abram'—that is, the parliamentarian Landa—who supported 'Julius'—that is, Stone.) The slogan on its masthead was 'Australia for the White Man'.

It maintained what it saw as time-honoured traditions. Between pink sepia covers, it continued to run the old favourite columns—Aboriginalities (about life in the bush), Smoke Oh (urban life), Business, Robbery etc. (finance), the Red Page (literature). The editors always had time for a beer in Fay's pub or a cup of coffee in Mockbell's and sometimes a swig of whisky with the comps down below. There was still the weekly cartoon conference and Wednesday afternoon off. 'Dad never missed an issue of the *Bully*!' people would say warmly to the dismayed staff, unaware that they were writing its obituary.

The staff would reassure each other that it took a war to sell the *Bully*. But circulation was tumbling (to something like half of its high of 70 000 during the war) and even its sister weekly, the *Women's Mirror*, could no longer cover its losses.

One of the most obvious signs of its collapse was the decline of its once popular cartoons. They drew on a great tradition—Hop, Phil May, Low, Dyson—that was now so exhausted that the jokes barely raised a smile. It would not be fair to blame the cartoonists entirely. The editorial impetus had also gone. The old Australian conservatism was dead and the *Bully* was going down with *Smith's Weekly* and *Truth*.

In 1950 it published a Jubilee issue, 'a *Bulletin* pageant'. Everyone was in it, from Joseph Furphy, Henry Lawson and Katharine Susannah Prichard to Gavin Casey, Brian James, Miles Franklin and Xavier Herbert. The poets ranged from Christopher Brennan, Shaw Neilson and 'Breaker' Morant to 'Banjo' Paterson, Hugh McCrae and R. D. Fitzgerald. It was a glittering achievement. It would have been a good moment to cease publication.

But magazines have their own momentum, even in decline. The old *Bully* soldiered on for another 10 years. Then its death throes finally engulfed the *Observer*.

CHAPTER 11
Last Days

One of Michael Baume's preoccupations in our business pages had been the adventures—and ethics—of the 'mortuary millionaires', the new takeover raiders. Now suddenly we became the shock troops of a takeover ourselves. Late in 1960 Australian Consolidated Press bought the *Bulletin* and, since it couldn't keep both magazines going, the end of the *Observer* was inevitable. Some half-hoped that Frank Packer would close the *Bulletin* and save the *Observer*, but he would no more have folded the legendary *Bulletin* than closed Angus & Robertson (if he had bought it). It would be like expecting Kerry Packer to close the *Sydney Morning Herald*. Possible but improbable. In any case the *Observer* was still a fragile coalition, and—we asked each other—were there not promising possibilities in a merger with a magazine that had so many poets, artists and critics in its circle?

Therefore, late in 1960, we packed up and moved from Elizabeth Street and Hyde Park down to the dark, Dantesque caverns of 252 George Street. The old *Bully* hands seemed to imagine us leaping from lorries and goosestepping through the corridors, led by Ober-Leutnant Donald Horne, with orders to take no prisoners. In fact we were more deferential than bellicose, as we slunk along the dun corridors and past the ancient peeling columns or stalagmites (as Douglas Stewart called them).

The *Bulletin* was still impressive. Ronald McCuaig was bringing out his *Bloodthirsty Bessie*. Stewart was reading proofs of his *Fisher's Ghost* and *Voyager Poems*. Among the contributors, Hal Porter, Brian James and Ethel Anderson were putting together collections of their *Bulletin* stories; Francis Webb and Ray Mathew, collections of their poems; Unk White and Eric Jolliffe, their cartoons and sketches. These were major talents at work, and Australia was the loser when this heritage was broken up.

The *Observer* went down fighting. In the last issues we covered in detail the final days of the old Angus & Robertson, in which I had a small and bizarre role. One morning shortly before we moved from Elizabeth Street, P. R. Stephensen, then employed by Walter Burns, the new managing director of Angus & Robertson, appeared with characteristic suddenness in my office and asked if I thought Frank Packer would like to buy A & R. Yes, I told him immediately, although I had no idea. Give him this telephone number, said Stephensen, scribbling on a tatty scrap of paper, and tell him to ring Burns. Packer did, but his takeover bid failed (and in due course Gordon Barton took it over).

A major controversy for and against Commonwealth subsidies for writers also blew up in our last issues. The novelist Olaf Ruhen was against them (they encouraged, he said, parasitism and 'avuncularism'). So was Max Harris ('sycophancy, lobbying, dishonesty'). But Douglas Stewart and Tom Inglis Moore defended the Commonwealth Literary Fund (on which they served). It was a classic exchange. Years later, when I tried to look again at this issue in *Quadrant* in the light of the massive expansion of government grants, I found that Max Harris may have been prophetic, since so many writers and artists who in conversation would speak out freely and loudly against the subsidisers were much too frightened to write the same criticisms down in signed articles. (One day no doubt someone will write a fat book, dedicated to Max Harris and Olaf Ruhen, demonstrating the harm that the system of subsidies and grants has done to Australian letters.)

This debate led to our final controversy. Olaf Ruhen had used Xavier Herbert's work to illustrate his case against subsidies. This in turn led to an historic contest between Herbert and P. R. Stephensen over the writing, editing and publishing of Herbert's famous novel, *Capricornia*. It will always remain a mystery how two such unreasonable and aggressive men were ever able to work together in the first place. Their angry polemics only ended when I refused to publish a libellous letter from Herbert. (Despite all my best efforts to promote Herbert's work, I was now consigned to the Herbertian outer darkness.)

At last the day came in March 1961 when the final issue of the *Observer* went to press in the basement of the *Bulletin* building. It had a fine—uncommissioned and unpaid—cover by Bob Hughes, made by blowing up a tiny dinkus he had drawn years before for about a dollar. The illustration was a fitting metaphor: tight-lipped, top-hatted undertakers carried a coffin from which emerged a jaunty hand, nonchalantly tapping ash from an elegant cigarette holder. The cover lines were: 'Or Death thy Victory?'

Perce Partridge, who had written so unfeelingly about the first issue, now wrote a cool appraisal of Jean-Paul Sartre's vulgar Marxism for the last. Alice Tay examined C. H. Rolph's (banned) book on the *Lady Chatterley's Lover* case. (She used the word 'fuck', never before used in a mainstream publication, not even yet in an acrostic. We decided that Packer company policy required us to observe the taboo.) Henry Mayer wrote on chastity, Frank Knöpfelmacher on communism, Ray Mathew on Kenneth Cook's *Wake in Fright*, Donald Horne on the future.

I wrote a memoir of the past three years. It touched on our early difficulty in settling on the right voice for our scepticism— for the liberal chic that dull critics called flip ('the sort of person who when God sounds the crack of doom will ask: Who is that smart aleck?') We had tried to combine libertarianism, anti-communism and multiculturalism. If we *were* flip, it was because we had lost patience with the cant of all parties, especially the progressives and leftists. Was it not better to be sometimes flip than always pompous and sanctimonious? I concluded that the best thing about the *Observer* was the unexpected alliances, the new coalition it expressed:

Without having planned anything of the kind, we found after the first year or so, that we had become a cooperative forum for

New Australians, rightwing trade unionists, radical Liberals, Melbourne Catholics, Sydney freethinkers . . . we helped discover and encourage a dialogue between these groups—the dialogue that offers the most promise for Australian culture.

Such was our happy illusion. We thought we owned the future. But no sooner had the *Observer* struck form than it was all over. Then, in accordance with publishing tradition, we gathered alongside the presses and, as the last issue began to roll, we shouted: 'Long live the *Observer*!' Something more than a magazine died.

For a brief period the new *Bulletin* was called the *Observer–Bulletin*. It was often brilliant. (It published, for example, the first of Amy Witting's Isobel stories that turned up 30 years later in the acclaimed novel *I for Isobel*.) But the two personalities could not be blended and the result appealed to few old readers of either magazine. *Bulletin* hands began to leave, including Douglas Stewart and Ronald McCuaig. This was the time Gwen Harwood wrote her famous acrostic farewelling the old *Bulletin* and rudely maledicting all editors. (Its principal consequence in the office was that Desmond O'Grady, the dramatist, novelist and new Red Page editor, spent more time reading poems for possible indecent acrostics—and finding some—than assessing their literary quality.)

The most dramatic departure was the last—M. H. Ellis's—by which time I was doing my stint as editor. I arranged a farewell dinner for him at the old baroque Belvedere Hotel (now a freeway tunnel) at Kings Cross. We all gave speeches—David McNicoll, Donald Horne and I—paying tribute to the old man, and Les Tanner sketched him. While Ellis was replying, we noticed that Frank Packer was sitting outside listening and smiling with curled lip. A seat was quickly found. He lumbered in, obviously not sober, and relit his cigar while grown men brushed the ash from his clothes. Ellis soon finished his remarks, and I asked Packer if he would care to say a few words. It was an unforgettable speech. He quietly and proudly sketched the history of Australian journalism in the twentieth century as a Packer family story: His father was one of the men who had founded *Smith's Weekly* and he later started the *Daily Guardian*. He himself had founded the *Australian Women's Weekly*, revived the *Daily Telegraph* and was now reviving the *Bulletin*. He had established Channel 9. His sons would do a thing or two.

Then with sudden rage he turned towards Ellis and shouted: 'But you bad-mouthed my father in the *Bulletin*! You said it was better for the Fairfaxes to buy the *Sun* than for the Packers to get it!' Ellis jumped to his feet: 'I didn't write that!' 'Yes you did! You wrote it in the *Bulletin*! In 1953!' Ellis shouted back: 'That wasn't me!' He named someone else. 'It *was* you!' Packer banged the table. The party broke up in confusion. I took Ellis to a taxi. It was an unfitting farewell to a great historian.

The end of the *Observer*, its merger with the *Bulletin*, was only one of the portents of the early 1960s. The whole circle, the new coalition in which I had invested so much, was dispersing. Everyone seemed to be leaving. Jim McAuley went to Hobart. Ray Mathew, Barry Humphries and Bruce Beresford to London. Robert Hughes to Manhattan. Harry Hooton died and with him the old bohemia. John Anderson retired and with him the old freethought. (There was at least one new arrival to give me some new hope—my second daughter.)

My own sense of things was changing. I had by now finished my book on censorship, tracing its serio-comic history in Australia from its cool and clumsy reception of Zola and de Maupassant in the 1880s through 'the heroic age' of the 1930s with its bans on James Joyce and George Orwell, on to the 1950s with its bans on J. D. Salinger, Mary McCarthy and Valdimir Nabokov (not to mention Max Harris or Robert Close in the 1940s). But if the details of this story were Dada, the theme was serious and my purpose in writing the book was to advance the total abolition of censorship of any kind. The book was called, in an Andersonian flourish, *Obscenity Blasphemy Sedition*.

The reviewers seemed delighted with the book and its chronicle of 100 awkward years of repression. Enthusiastic enemies of all forms of censorship like the late Senator Lionel Murphy sent me warm letters of congratulation.

But I had no sooner finished writing it than I began to question its assumptions. In the end I let it go and reserved second thoughts for a later edition. At issue was far more than the use of a few obscene words. What had begun in the nineteenth century as a crusade for freedom of thought and literature, or even simply of information, had become a bandwagon for a new coarseness and nihilism—which, following Berkeley's Dirty Speech Movement, could easily be elaborated into a political cause.

My new view was that a minimal censorship preserved the capacity of the community to express, however symbolically, a protest, a gesture, against degradation. Ordinary people readily agreed with this idea, quaint as it seems today. But 20 years ago liberals or liberationists treated any defence of censorship with contempt. Probably the only thing more disgusting in their sight was the spectacle of someone becoming a born-again Christian.

None of my writings in this populist vein appeared to influence anybody at all. I began to feel I had reached a dead end, that the cause was doomed—a view often enough strengthened by the stupidity of so many of the conservatives I had begun to defend. For example, no sooner had I begun working out my second thoughts on censorship than the Chief Secretary of New South Wales banned an early film by Bruce Beresford and Albie Thoms based on a Dada ballet by Jacques Prévert which showed God, in disgust with the world, defecating on a black-tie party in Sydney. It was impossible not to despise this sort of exercise of authority—let alone the prosecutions about this time of OZ magazine over Martin Sharp's clever satires of the more fatuous aspects of suburban life. A magistrate actually sentenced Sharp to prison, along with his editors, Richard Walsh and Richard Neville, and the printer, Francis James (although all the sentences were quashed on appeal.)

If this was conservatism, I was certainly not part of it; and if liberalism mandated pornography, I was no longer a liberal. Where then was I? I had no answer, but it was clear that the inevitable abolition of censorship did not herald a new age of freedom. New battle lines were being drawn, as the old Vice Squad began to withdraw and the new Thought Police took up their positions. Today a totally new version of *Obscenity Blasphemy Sedition* is waiting to be written.

I also felt this note of uncertainty or foreboding in the symposium, *Australian Civilisation*, which I was then editing. Everything began cheerfully enough. The Melbourne publisher, Andrew Fabinyi, rang me at my office in the *Observer* and said he had an idea he wanted to talk to me about, maybe over lunch. The idea was that I bring together a number of *Observer* contributors, intellectuals of broadly liberal disposition, for a 'symposium' about where Australia was going as it entered a new and promising decade. The book would be called *Australian Civilisation*.

The timing was right. Almost everyone agreed that large but undebated changes were taking place in the country—for better or worse. For some, there was a new surge of Australian nationality. For others, a new age of irony and urbanity. For everybody there was an 'end of ideology'. Andrew Fabinyi gave me *carte blanche* and anyone I approached—from Vincent Buckley and Max Harris to Sol Encel and Donald Horne—immediately agreed to join in the symposium. One or two—Robert Hughes, for example, even pushed in, gatecrashing the party as it were. It was an idea whose moment had come.

We settled on a simple approach. We would for once outstare the Medusa's head of Australian philistinism and confront the dark side of democracy. With luck we might also help elaborate an Australian liberalism for the 1960s. It had not occurred to us—or most of us—to ask questions about the death of God. Manning Clark, in his chapter 'Faith', did ask these questions. In fact he challenged the ground plan of the whole symposium, if not sabotaged it entirely. But I did not see this at the time, and none of the reviewers noticed it.

I was delighted to get Manning Clark at all. He was at the

height of his powers—he had written but not yet published the first and best volume of his *A History of Australia*—and he had not yet succumbed to his 'fatal flaw', the demagoguery that would devalue so much of his later work.

When I called on him one evening in Canberra, he was engrossed in a television screening of Carol Reed's famous film scripted by Graham Greene, *The Third Man*. It was the moment when Harry Lime, the callous, genial criminal played by Orson Welles, delivered his famous speech from the Great Wheel in the bombed Viennese pleasure garden. In Renaissance Italy, Harry Lime said, the Borgias brought not only murder and war but also Leonardo da Vinci. But what have Switzerland's 500 years of liberalism produced? . . . The cuckoo clock! Clark sat fascinated and silently beckoned me to a chair. When the scene was over he nodded, speechless with admiration.

In our discussion he had about him very much the air of a man in crisis who might at any moment leap the secular–humanist fence and seek reception into the Church. As late as 1958, in an essay on the Portuguese explorer Quiros, he had declared that the Christian faith would surely rise triumphant from the ashes of Australian secularism. Was he, you could not help asking, engaged in the same spiritual drama James McAuley had embodied ten years earlier?

The essay he finally gave me for the symposium outlined for the first time the great theme of Volume 1 of his *History*—the tensions and accommodations within Australia of Protestantism, Catholicism and the Enlightenment. But it was his discussion of the Enlightenment that struck at the heart of our enterprise, and reverberates today. It is still in my mind throughout these chapters.

He began with the widely held idea that the struggle for the future of Australia would not be between the Christians and the godless, but between the two branches of godless liberalism represented in the book. (In a *jeu d'esprit* he gave these branches a geographical dimension, centring one in Melbourne and the other in Sydney. This ingenious stroke endowed popular regionalism with a spiritual depth few had imagined and stimulated a certain amount of earnest scholarship for a time).

Clark described the first of the two branches variously as progressives, social democrats, meliorists, interventionists, liberationists, or Men of the Future. The second were sceptics, elitists, adventurists, stoics, Nietzscheans, even Heracleiteans. Most of us call them liberals and conservatives, or left and right.

But Clark's argument went much further still: these two secular movements, now rubbing along in the sort of consensus that sustained *Australian Civilisation*, must soon become irreconcilable as liberals on the left turned to revolution and conservatives on the right to the Church. The future, he wrote, lies either with the Men of 1917 or with Christ. This will be the final struggle for Australia.

1917! Did he mean by this a sort of anarchic but creative revolutionism that some saw in Russsia before the Thermidorean reaction under Stalin—the era of Mayakovsky? But no, it was clear he did not. He meant the straitjacket of Stalinism. Extraordinarily, he wrote in this vein when Soviet suppression in 1956 of Hungarian writers, intellectuals and workers was fresh in memory, and when in Australia as elsewhere its members were abandoning the Communist Party in droves. Later, as the truth about the Soviet Union became obvious even to the dullest observer, he might turn to revolution in a broader, vaguer sense, but he never concealed the idea that blood would stain the wattle. Indeed he seemed to enjoy the prospect.

What did he mean by the Christian alternative to 1917? Generally he had in mind James McAuley, his slightly younger contemporary whose influence on him was always strong. Despite fundamental disagreements, the two writers had much in common, and the best way to judge the early Clark is to read him as a mirror image of McAuley. Both felt at that period a revulsion from the disinherited, secular world—the Kingdom of Nothingness (Clark) or the realm of sterility (McAuley). Both had an apocalyptic sense of the future and both sought guidance in the past.

The poet and the historian understood each other. When, for

example, an angry controversy broke out in the *Bulletin* over Volume 1 of *A History of Australia*, McAuley was determined that *Quadrant* should not join the attack but find a reviewer who could enter into the turmoil of Clark's mind. (It was Michael Roe.) He himself reviewed *Meeting Soviet Man* with patience.

For his part, Clark recognised in McAuley's *Captain Quiros* a sketch of the epic history he might have written if he had not turned, in 'desperation', to the ideas of 1917. In McAuley's poem, Quiros' dying vision traces Australian history from the Spanish, Dutch and English explorers to the first colonisers, from the slaughter of Aborigines to the persecution of Christian believers, from democracy and liberalism to the coming triumph of communism when the faithful will die wretched and alone:

> They shall drink horror, suffer all mishap,
> And see their Mother seated upon earth
> In human weakness, holding in her lap
> The head of Antichrist, her own misbirth.

None of this was part of our scheme for *Australian Civilisation*. Yet Clark's chapter, like Volume 1 of his *History* and McAuley's *Captain Quiros*, challenged my view of things, then and later. There was for me, however, no turning again to the revolution that had confounded my adolescent years after the war. I had absorbed too much from George Orwell, Malcolm Muggeridge, Bertrand Russell and dozens of those who had been to hell and back—Silone, Max Eastman, Ante Ciliga, Arthur Koestler.

One or two of my circle in these earlier years may have still looked to Barcelona of 1937 (the anarchists) or to Belgrade of 1947 (the Titoists) or even to John Anderson's revolutionary stoicism or classicism. But the communists! It was unthinkable. We might have argued tediously about the rights and wrongs of conscription in the Korean War, but everyone agreed that the communists must be defeated. Or argued forever about how best to oppose the Menzies government's plans to ban communism, but everyone agreed that the Communist Party and the Nazi Party were twins. Some of us took it for granted that Hitler had won the war in the guise of Stalin.

As for the Church, too many generations of liberalism had weakened its appeal for me. I envied the faithful but I could not follow them. However much I responded to McAuley's passionate essays in *The End of Modernity*, I sympathised with Irving Kristol who, when trying to write a review of it in New York, finally tore his draft to shreds and flung the book across the room. (In later years Kristol came around to agreeing with McAuley after all.)

For my part I would continue a fellow-traveller of secular liberalism, making what I could of its resources, keeping one step ahead of the Hound of Heaven. But I could never think of liberalism in the same way again, although I tried to.

It still seemed to me then, as now, that there was more than a sterile Kingdom of Nothingness in the way of life which some called bourgeois or suburban or liberal or even British but which was plainly Australian—and sufficiently free, peaceful and prosperous to seem almost utopian to many foreigners. No doubt it lacked spiritual depth and could no longer be called a Christian society. But that might compel us to examine its secular traditions and institutions for keys to its comparative success.

Australian Civilisation, including Manning Clark's subversive chapter, was well received. Apart from some easily predicted men of malice, the critics liked the book and it ran into several editions. But it was the last of the symposiums in which people who disagreed on great issues could still talk to each other civilly. We were entering a new period of intolerance.

PART FOUR

Debacle

C'est inutile de se donner tant mal à la tête pour n'arriver qu'à changer d'erreur.

(It is pointless to give oneself such a bad headache only to end up changing one's mistakes.)

Ernest Renan

CHAPTER 12

God and Man in Sydney

In July 1961, not long after the *Bulletin* had absorbed the *Observer*, it became one of my jobs to keep a journalistic eye on a convention of lawyers who were then assembling in their hundreds from around the world. For me, it ended up in a sort of fiasco that became another turning point in my life.

The convention was an august occasion. The Lord Mayor of Sydney and a Minister of the Crown representing the Premier welcomed the lawyers and their wives at a reception in the Town Hall and His Excellency the Governor of New South Wales presided over the opening ceremony at which the Sydney Symphony Orchestra, Joseph Mozart Post conducting, played suitable items—a little Berlioz and Dvorak but mainly Australian composers Percy Grainger (*Molly on the Shore*), Arthur Benjamin (*Old English Dances*) and Alfred Hill (*The Moon's Gold Horn*).

In the course of the week the lawyers debated anything from murder to federalism. Their programme also included a buffet dinner on the harbour and a dinner dance at the Trocadero as well as golf, bowls and tennis for the sportsmen. At the final ceremonial dinner at David Jones', the president produced the loving cup and proposed the first of various toasts to the profession throughout the common law world. The Prime Minister R. G. Menzies responded. The ladies attended a theatre party, Somerset Maugham's *The Constant Wife*, starring Googie Withers.

But the most remarkable of the events was a service in a packed Anglican Cathedral Church of St Andrew at 9 a.m. on the day after the opening ceremony. Journalists had been tipped off to expect something unusual, but few foresaw the furore that followed the sermon of the Anglican Primate, Archbishop H. R. Gough, an Englishman in the evangelical tradition.

From my pew I had a good view of the the arrival of the eminent lawyers including the Lord Chief Justice of England, Lord Parker of Waddington; the Chief Justice of the United States, Earl Warren; the Chief Justice of Australia, Sir Owen Dixon; and the Chief Justice of New South Wales, Dr Herbert Vere Evatt. When they were seated, everyone including journalists and a few lawyers unfamiliar with Anglican forms of worship joined in singing as best they could:

> Frail children of dust
> And feeble as frail,
> In Thee do we trust
> Nor find Thee to fail.

A bishop led us in confession. Then following the singing of the Benedictus (*Blessed be the Lord God of Israel*), the President of the Law Council of Australia read the first lesson—from Job ('But where shall wisdom be found?') and the Governor of New South Wales read the second lesson—from Matthew ('Judge not that ye be not judged'). Prayers followed—for the blessing of our Sovereign Lady, Queen Elizabeth; for the meting out of His eternal justice in our courts of law; for the kindling of the true love of peace in the hearts of all men—concluding with the Lord's Prayer.

The moment for the sermon arrived and journalists leaned forward. Speaking in a clipped, high-pitched voice, the archbishop took as his theme the consequences of the loss of belief in God. His principal illustration was the recent trial in Israel of Adolf Eichmann, who had administered the Holocaust in the Third Reich, uninhibited by the voice of conscience that had become in the words of the New Testament 'seared with a hot iron'.

Communism has the same searing effect on conscience, he noted, well aware that the assembly included Lord Parker, who had only the other day in London sentenced George Blake to 42 years' imprisonment for spying for Russia—'one of the worst cases that can be envisaged', Lord Parker told Blake, 'other than in time of war'.

The archbishop appealed to the legal profession to do all that it could 'to strengthen moral principles of conduct' and not to give way to 'the popular clamour to relax the severity of the law'. In particular he scorned the current slogan of despair: 'Better Red than Dead'. It was far better, he said, to die a free man than to live as a slave.

So far the Primate had not moved far beyond what most of his listeners, including the reporters, had expected. The reporters welcomed the bit about not relaxing the law's severity. It was what you wanted from an archbishop. But was this all the copy they could expect to get? But the material for headlines soon followed. Turning closer to home, the Primate warned the assembled lawyers that materialist doctrines, which are the source of totalitarian atheism, were being taught in Australian schools of philosophy, even here in Sydney (where for over 30 years John Anderson and his disciples had taught a doctrine of freethought) '. . . yes even here in Sydney, we have those who are shamelessly teaching in our universities these same soul-destroying philosophies. I am not saying these lecturers are communists but they are teaching ideas which are breaking down the restraints of conscience, decrying the institution of marriage, urging our students to premarital sexual experience, advocating free love and the right of self-expression.'

The reporters were delighted and some perhaps sang the offertory hymn with real feeling: 'Praise to the Lord, who doth prosper thy work'. After they had all filed out to the cathedral steps, the photographers jostled to snap the judges, especially Lord Parker, congratulating the archbishop.

But any euphoria was soon buried in controversy. It turned out that His Grace had relied heavily on a polemic *Empiricism and Freedom* written and distributed by Dr Kinsella, a Roman Catholic doctor of medicine who, believing that ideas have consequences, was convinced that secularist ideas had plainly observable evil consequences:

> The 'philosophy' fed to our youth by the Sydney University is *rubbish*. It is devoid of strength and manliness, but contains the seeds of moral corruption and political subversion. The [University] Senate should give an account of its stewardship in this matter. Can the community afford the folly of feeding this atheistic materialism to the elite of its youth, year after year, through generation after generation of students? Can the Senate be sure there will be no retribution?

Never one for half-measures, he wanted to close down the sociology department at the University of New South Wales and he called on the Vice Squad to investigate the philosophy department at the University of Sydney. Perhaps, he thought, the Crown should be advised to withdraw the Royal Charter from Sydney University altogether.

The archbishop had not gone so far, but he had raised this question: 'If it is true that empires and nations have fallen because of moral corruption which has sapped the mental vitality and physical strength of the people, *is it not the duty of governments* to take note of this decline in morals and to *take action*?'

In the subsequent controversy, many were quick to criticise the archbishop. Neither Dr Gough nor Dr Kinsella was a philosopher. Neither understood John Anderson's metaphysical empiricism (which had as one of its eccentric characteristics a belief in the objective reality of good and evil totally independent of our ideas of right and wrong) or seemed aware that he had been one of the few active critics of Marxism and communism in Sydney University in the post-war years when Stalin's fellow-travellers were most influential.

Many men of the Church distanced themselves from the Primate. Dr Felix Arnott, the Warden of St Paul's College (and later Archbishop of Brisbane) thought he was 'grossly misinformed'. The Dean of Melbourne, Dr S. Barton Babbage, observed that when an academic's freedom of speech is curtailed, 'the next step is the rubber truncheon and the concentration camp'. In an editorial in the *Anglican*, Francis James described the homily as 'grossly and gratuitously insulting'.

One or two lawyers deplored the archbishop's sense of occasion. A convention of Chief Justices, Queen's Counsel and learned lawyers was not the forum in which to allege unsubstantiated charges which 'would not last two minutes in court'.

Several academics were contemptuous of the archbishop's call for some sort of state supervision, if not intervention. The Vice Chancellor of Sydney, an historian, recalled the swinging 1920s and the defeatist 1930s and in his opinion the students of Sydney University now were morally superior to their predecessors. Officers of academics' unions demanded that the archbishop apologise for his 'smears'. Student leaders said their constituents were not immoral but boring, suburban and conventional. A communist spokesman announced that a deputation from the party would wait on the Primate to advise him that the Soviet Union was sexually pure and to explain the principles of co-existence.

The press was divided. The Packer press, or at least its flagship, the *Daily Telegraph*, remained editorially aloof if not neutral. The Murdoch press judicially called for more evidence. But the Fairfax press, with one or two qualifications, supported the archbishop: he had at last raised to the point of public confrontation the uncompromising clash between the conservatism of the Sydney establishment, represented by Warwick Fairfax, and the modernist radicalism, represented by John Anderson.

Anderson and Fairfax had never concealed their distaste or even contempt for each other's position. The conflict began some 34 years earlier, in 1927—the same year in which John Anderson assumed his Chair as Challis Professor of Philosophy and Warwick Fairfax became a director of John Fairfax & Sons Ltd.

The issue then was the case of Sacco and Vanzetti, two Italian anarchists who were executed in Massachusetts for murder. There is little doubt today that Sacco was guilty, but no doubt that neither of them received a fair trial. There were well coordinated protests in capital cities around the world which led to riots in Buenos Aires and bombings in Paris and Barcelona. In Sydney, the Communist Party and the Seamen's Union organised a procession from Eddy Avenue along George Street to the Cenotaph, where hundreds of men and women observed two minutes' silence in honour of their 'judicially murdered comrades' (as Jock Garden put it), and then marched on to the Domain to join hundreds of other protesters.

In its leader the *Sydney Morning Herald* declared that Sacco and Vanzetti had exhaustively pursued all judicial steps available to them under the American system of justice. They had, it concluded, been properly found guilty of murder. The demonstrators were ignorant sheep led by insincere demagogues.

Anderson immediately sent a letter to the *Sydney Morning Herald*: the principal issue which the demonstrators were raising, he wrote, was not the guilt or innocence of the executed men but the allegation of a frame-up within the judicial system. The protesters believed the trials were unfair. But the *Sydney Morning Herald* did not seriously examine this issue.

The newspaper published this letter, but it rejected two further letters Anderson wrote in the course of the controversy. When he sought an explanation, the editor informed him that the *Sydney Morning Herald* needed the space for *news*. Since so much of the news published had been concealed comment, Anderson treated the explanation as the pious humbug characteristic of conservatives when lying. He never wrote again for the *Sydney Morning Herald*: 'The whole episode gave me a lesson in ethics which I shall not readily forget.'

But the *Sydney Morning Herald* continued to attack him throughout the following decades. In 1931 when Anderson publicly derided political superstitions (patriotism) and idols (war memorials), the *Herald*—of which Warwick Fairfax was now managing director—considered such opinions to be 'in highly doubtful taste' and supported a parliamentary motion condemning them as 'not in accordance with the national sentiment'. Liberty, the *Herald* said, is not licence, and freedom must be restricted 'in the interests of society'. (The Sydney University senate supported the *Herald* against its professor and passed a motion censuring Anderson.)

In 1943 when Anderson denounced the role of religion and the churches in education, the *Herald* was fork-tongued: as a citizen, it declared, Anderson had the right to his opinions, subject to the law of blasphemy or sedition; but if, as the head of a university faculty, he acted contrary to his responsibilities, the university senate should take appropriate action against him.

The more the Fairfax press—and Warwick Fairfax himself in occasional signed essays—appealed to the necessity for restraints on freedom of speech, to the demands of good taste, and to the imperatives of the ethic of service, the more contemptuous Anderson became. The student, he would thunder to freshers, has the right to be as obscene, blasphemous or seditious as he likes! (I can vouch for the breath of fresh air this brought to at least one 17-year-old oppressed by pious cant and self-serving lies.)

Inevitably when Fairfax began developing his metaphysical ideas—first in the manuscript of the 1950s *The Twain Shall Meet* (God and man, East and West) which he circulated to friends, and then in the book *The Triple Abyss* (the abyss, that is, between man, God and eternity)—Anderson was totally dismissive (although his follower, the theologically trained G. Stuart Watts, whom I persuaded to review it for the *Bulletin*, was more respectful). For his part, Fairfax did not claim to be a pedagogic or academic philosopher: he always let it be noted in *Who's Who* that his Oxford degree was a second.

But his book was a lifetime's reflections on life and death, not a crib for undergraduates. It was also a polemic against the empiricism and materialism that Anderson had been teaching in Sydney since his arrival.

In the 1950s Fairfax had three of his plays produced in Sydney, all exploring the theme of passion versus convention, and all acknowledging the claims of both. Anderson again was totally dismissive and contrasted them with James Joyce's play *Exiles*, which has the same theme but fights it out, or tries to, without compromise.

On those rare occasions when Anderson and Fairfax found themselves on the same side, for example in opposition to the Soviet Union and the Communist Party in the Cold War, there was little sense of real agreement. Even in his most conservative mood, Anderson despised the philistine Sydney establishment. At the time of the Margaret Street riot in 1947, when students were demonstrating in support of Indonesia's declaration of independence, the *Herald* gave the highest priority to its criticism of the police and their mishandling of the demonstration. Anderson ridiculed the *Herald*'s misjudgment: of course the police must be criticised, but the real issue of the day was the Russian threat to the world. Later, when the Menzies Government decided to dissolve the Communist Party, the *Herald* supported the government but Anderson opposed it—as 'an act of colossal folly' and a reversion to rule by proscription and regulation.

But despite over 30 years of conflict on particular issues between the Fairfax press and Anderson, the *Herald* had never been involved in a direct attack on Anderson's school as a whole until the archbishop's sermon to the lawyers.

The Fairfax afternoon *Sun* was 'profoundly disturbed' by the archbishop's disclosures but the *Sydney Morning Herald* was more judicious. It knew that the weak links in the camapign were Dr Kinsella's philosophic analysis, which no one took seriously, and Dr Gough's call for government action, which alarmed most liberals and academics. But the *Herald* congratulated the archbishop on his courage in bringing the scandal of the universities to public attention. Certainly, it conceded, 'his zeal and his passionate anxiety to strengthen religious values in a Christian society under constant pressure from materialist forces' had led him into exaggerations. 'But a great many people share his conviction that the predominance of the philosophy of empiricism in our universities has led to a serious weakening of those values.'

The *Sydney Morning Herald* also opened its pages to debate on the issue and by the volume of letters it published, the newspaper, as much as the archbishop, created the controversy. Since Anderson had only shortly before retired, his followers saw the whole campaign as a kind of vindictive valedictory.

The polemics continued for some weeks, but few if any seemed willing to come to the issue which the archbishop had so badly, even crudely, raised—the influence of the spirit of secularism ('godless atheism') on the way we live now. The legal convention finished and the judges and learned counsel left Sydney behind them, without having contributed a word to the public debate. A recently established government inquiry into youth examined the matter briefly but decided there was 'insufficient evidence' and quickly passed on without looking for any.

One or two philosophers noted that, under the influence of philosophy, some students, like the distraught youth in McAuley's autobiographical poem, appeared to 'wander the earth without vocation'. One or two schoolteachers, including Alastair Mackerras, later a widely honoured headmaster of Sydney Grammar, also broke ranks: surely, he asked, the denial of the existence of right and wrong must have *some* influence on conduct?

The affair was about to fizzle out in abusive stalemate when the retiring president of the students' council, Peter Wilenski, thought of one final act. He invited John Anderson to return to his old university and address the students. The sixties generation was just beginning to flex its muscles. Students in their hundreds packed the hall or milled outside waiting to catch a glimpse of the man they had never heard speak but whom they were now beginning to see as a legendary precursor of the new liberation.

Anderson for his part had just finished revising his last major paper, 'Classicism'. It was his intellectual testament and in it he poured the scorn, accumulated from a lifetime of argument and reflection, on modernity and its associated progressivism, democratism, and optimism. The spirit of the age, he said, was 'sickly', 'debilitating', 'contaminating', 'woolly minded'. Wherever he looked, there was a falling of educational standards, a 'slighter and slighter *literacy*' among the supposedly educated. A classicist must see the resemblances today with the classical Greece in its decline. It may be indeed that our modern age, dating from the Renaissance, is on the verge of collapse before a new barbarism shown by indifference to standards, hostility to traditions, contempt for elites, and distortion of subjects by liberationism.

He concluded 'Classicism' with a warning against the new spirit of *fear*—especially the fear of *criticising* democracy and the fear of giving offence to the multitude: 'for, as Socrates says in the *Crito*, though "the many may kill us", that is no reason for setting their opinions on a level with the wise, for believing, though they have a certain power over life and death, that they have any power over truth'.

But this was not the message he delivered to the hundreds of cheering students when he arrived back at Sydney University. After an early reference to Socrates, whom he had always presented as the freethinker's alternative to Christ, he remembered the archbishop, Warwick Fairfax and the *Sydney Morning Herald* and quickly moved on to denounce religious superstition ('at least as dangerous as loose living'), ecclesiastical interference with academic freedom, and the general decline in the idea of university self-government as illustrated by the indifference of so many academics to the 'rank frame-up' of Professor Orr.

The gales of laughter and the tumultuous applause that greeted the philosopher's sallies so distressed those standing outside and unable to hear that, halfway through the proceedings, a pathetic note was passed on to the chairman pleading for insiders to press a little closer together so that some outsiders might squeeze in.

The churches and the universities will always be incompatible, Anderson continued, his speech and eyes now ignited. Students and academics have a duty to resist clerical encroachments. 'If religious